Sometimes I ain't so sho who's got ere a right to say when a man is crazy and when he ain't. Sometimes I think it ain't none of us pure crazy and ain't none of us pure sane until the balance of us talks him that-a-way. It's like it ain't so much what a fellow does, but it's the way the majority of folks is looking at him when he does it.

William Faulkner, *AS I LAY DYING*

Acknowledgments

Four chapters of this book originally appeared in slightly different form elsewhere. Chapter 3 appeared in the *American Journal of Sociology*, LIX (November, 1953); Chapter 5 appeared in the same journal, LVII (September, 1951). Both are reprinted here with the permission of the *Journal* and the University of Chicago Press. Chapter 4 appeared in *Human Organization*, 12 (Spring, 1953), and is reprinted here with the permission of the Society for Applied Anthropology. Chapter 6 appeared in *Social Problems*, 3 (July, 1955), and is reprinted with the permission of the Society for the Study of Social Problems.

The material in Chapters 3 and 4 was originally prepared

as a Master's thesis in Sociology at the University of Chicago, under the direction of Everett C. Hughes, W. Lloyd Warner, and Harvey L. Smith. Dan C. Lortie commented on an early draft of one of the papers.

I did the research on which Chapters 5 and 6 are based while I was a member of the staff of the Chicago Narcotics Survey, a project undertaken by the Chicago Area Projects, Inc., with the help of a grant from the National Institute of Mental Health. Harold Finestone, Eliot Freidson, Erving Goffman, Solomon Kobrin, Henry McKay, Anselm Strauss, and the late R. Richard Wohl criticized early versions of these papers.

I am greatly indebted to Blanche Geer, who read and discussed several versions of the entire manuscript with me. My thinking on questions of deviance, as on all matters sociological, owes much to my friend and teacher, Everett C. Hughes.

Dorothy Seelinger, Kathryn James, and Lois Stoops typed the several versions of the manuscript with patience and care.

Contents

1 Outsiders

ALL social groups make rules and attempt, at some times and under some circumstances, to enforce them. Social rules define situations and the kinds of behavior appropriate to them, specifying some actions as "right" and forbidding others as "wrong." When a rule is enforced, the person who is supposed to have broken it may be seen as a special kind of person, one who cannot be trusted to live by the rules agreed on by the group. He is regarded as an *outsider*.

But the person who is thus labeled an outsider may have a different view of the matter. He may not accept the rule by which he is being judged and may not regard those who judge him as either competent or legitimately entitled to do so. Hence, a second meaning of the term emerges: the rule-breaker may feel his judges are *outsiders*.

In what follows, I will try to clarify the situation and process pointed to by this double-barrelled term: the situations of rule-breaking and rule-enforcement and the processes by which some people come to break rules and others to enforce them.

Some preliminary distinctions are in order. Rules may be of a great many kinds. They may be formally enacted into law, and in this case the police power of the state may be used in enforcing them. In other cases, they represent informal agreements, newly arrived at or encrusted with the sanction of age and tradition; rules of this kind are enforced by informal sanctions of various kinds.

Similarly, whether a rule has the force of law or tradition or is simply the result of consensus, it may be the task of some specialized body, such as the police or the committee on ethics of a professional association, to enforce it; enforcement, on the other hand, may be everyone's job or, at least, the job of everyone in the group to which the rule is meant to apply.

Many rules are not enforced and are not, in any except the most formal sense, the kind of rules with which I am concerned. Blue laws, which remain on the statute books though they have not been enforced for a hundred years, are examples. (It is important to remember, however, that an unenforced law may be reactivated for various reasons and regain all its original force, as recently occurred with respect to the laws governing the opening of commercial establishments on Sunday in Missouri.) Informal rules may similarly die from lack of enforcement. I shall mainly be concerned with what we can call the actual operating rules of groups, those kept alive through attempts at enforcement.

Finally, just how far "outside" one is, in either of the senses I have mentioned, varies from case to case. We think of the person who commits a traffic violation or gets a little too drunk at a party as being, after all, not very different from the rest of us and treat his infraction tolerantly. We regard the thief as less like us and punish him severely. Crimes such as murder, rape, or treason lead us to view the violator as a true outsider.

In the same way, some rule-breakers do not think they have been unjustly judged. The traffic violator usually subscribes to the very rules he has broken. Alcoholics are often ambivalent, sometimes feeling that those who judge them do not understand them and at other times agreeing that compulsive drinking is a bad thing. At the extreme, some deviants (homosexuals and drug addicts are good examples) develop full-blown ideologies explaining why they are right and why those who disapprove of and punish them are wrong.

Definitions of Deviance

The outsider—the deviant from group rules—has been the subject of much speculation, theorizing, and scientific study. What laymen want to know about deviants is: why do they do it? How can we account for their rule-breaking? What is there about them that leads them to do forbidden things? Scientific research has tried to find answers to these questions. In doing so it has accepted the common-sense premise that there is something inherently deviant (qualitatively distinct) about acts that break (or seem to break) social rules. It has also accepted the common-sense assumption that the deviant act occurs because some characteristic of the person who commits it makes it necessary or inevitable that he should. Scientists do not ordinarily question the label "deviant"

3

when it is applied to particular acts or people but rather take it as given. In so doing, they accept the values of the group making the judgment.

It is easily observable that different groups judge different things to be deviant. This should alert us to the possibility that the person making the judgment of deviance, the process by which that judgment is arrived at, and the situation in which it is made may all be intimately involved in the phenomenon of deviance. To the degree that the common-sense view of deviance and the scientific theories that begin with its premises assume that acts that break rules are inherently deviant and thus take for granted the situations and processes of judgment, they may leave out an important variable. If scientists ignore the variable character of the process of judgment, they may by that omission limit the kinds of theories that can be developed and the kind of understanding that can be achieved.[1]

Our first problem, then, is to construct a definition of deviance. Before doing this, let us consider some of the definitions scientists now use, seeing what is left out if we take them as a point of departure for the study of outsiders.

The simplest view of deviance is essentially statistical, defining as deviant anything that varies too widely from the average. When a statistician analyzes the results of an agricultural experiment, he describes the stalk of corn that is exceptionally tall and the stalk that is exceptionally short as deviations from the mean or average. Similarly, one can describe anything that differs from what is most common as a deviation. In this view, to be left-handed or redheaded is deviant, because most people are right-handed and brunette.

So stated, the statistical view seems simple-minded, even

1. Cf. Donald R. Cressey, "Criminological Research and the Definition of Crimes," *American Journal of Sociology*, LVI (May, 1951), 546-551.

trivial. Yet it simplifies the problem by doing away with many questions of value that ordinarily arise in discussions of the nature of deviance. In assessing any particular case, all one need do is calculate the distance of the behavior involved from the average. But it is too simple a solution. Hunting with such a definition, we return with a mixed bag—people who are excessively fat or thin, murderers, redheads, homosexuals, and traffic violators. The mixture contains some ordinarily thought of as deviants and others who have broken no rule at all. The statistical definition of deviance, in short, is too far removed from the concern with rule-breaking which prompts scientific study of outsiders.

A less simple but much more common view of deviance identifies it as something essentially pathological, revealing the presence of a "disease." This view rests, obviously, on a medical analogy. The human organism, when it is working efficiently and experiencing no discomfort, is said to be "healthy." When it does not work efficiently, a disease is present. The organ or function that has become deranged is said to be pathological. Of course, there is little disagreement about what constitutes a healthy state of the organism. But there is much less agreement when one uses the notion of pathology analogically, to describe kinds of behavior that are regarded as deviant. For people do not agree on what constitutes healthy behavior. It is difficult to find a definition that will satisfy even such a select and limited group as psychiatrists; it is impossible to find one that people generally accept as they accept criteria of health for the organism.[2]

Sometimes people mean the analogy more strictly, because they think of deviance as the product of mental disease. The

2. See the discussion in C. Wright Mills, "The Professional Ideology of Social Pathologists," *American Journal of Sociology*, XLIX (September, 1942), 165–180.

behavior of a homosexual or drug addict is regarded as the symptom of a mental disease just as the diabetic's difficulty in getting bruises to heal is regarded as a symptom of his disease. But mental disease resembles physical disease only in metaphor:

Starting with such things as syphilis, tuberculosis, typhoid fever, and carcinomas and fractures, we have created the class "illness." At first, this class was composed of only a few items, all of which shared the common feature of reference to a state of disordered structure or function of the human body as a physio-chemical machine. As time went on, additional items were added to this class. They were not added, however, because they were newly discovered bodily disorders. The physician's attention had been deflected from this criterion and had become focused instead on disability and suffering as new criteria for selection. Thus, at first slowly, such things as hysteria, hypochondriasis, obsessive-complusive neurosis, and depression were added to the category of illness. Then, with increasing zeal, physicians and especially psychiatrists began to call "illness" (that is, of course, "mental illness") anything and everything in which they could detect any sign of malfunctioning, based on no matter what norm. Hence, agoraphobia is illness because one should not be afraid of open spaces. Homosexuality is illness because heterosexuality is the social norm. Divorce is illness because it signals failure of marriage. Crime, art, undesired political leadership, participation in social affairs, or withdrawal from such participation—all these and many more have been said to be signs of mental illness.[3]

The medical metaphor limits what we can see much as the statistical view does. It accepts the lay judgment of something as deviant and, by use of analogy, locates its source within the individual, thus preventing us from seeing the judgment itself as a crucial part of the phenomenon.

3. Thomas Szasz, *The Myth of Mental Illness* (New York: Paul B. Hoeber, Inc., 1961), pp. 44-45; see also Erving Goffman, "The Medical Model and Mental Hospitalization," in *Asylums: Essays on the Social Situation of Mental Patients and Other Inmates* (Garden City: Anchor Books, 1961), pp. 321-386.

Some sociologists also use a model of deviance based essentially on the medical notions of health and disease. They look at a society, or some part of a society, and ask whether there are any processes going on in it that tend to reduce its stability, thus lessening its chance of survival. They label such processes deviant or identify them as symptoms of social disorganization. They discriminate between those features of society which promote stability (and thus are "functional") and those which disrupt stability (and thus are "dysfunctional"). Such a view has the great virtue of pointing to areas of possible trouble in a society of which people may not be aware.[4]

But it is harder in practice than it appears to be in theory to specify what is functional and what dysfunctional for a society or social group. The question of what the purpose or goal (function) of a group is and, consequently, what things will help or hinder the achievement of that purpose, is very often a political question. Factions within the group disagree and maneuver to have their own definition of the group's function accepted. The function of the group or organization, then, is decided in political conflict, not given in the nature of the organization. If this is true, then it is likewise true that the questions of what rules are to be enforced, what behavior regarded as deviant, and which people labeled as outsiders must also be regarded as political.[5] The functional view of deviance, by ignoring the political aspect of the phenomenon, limits our understanding.

Another sociological view is more relativistic. It identifies

4. See Robert K. Merton, "Social Problems and Sociological Theory," in Robert K. Merton and Robert A. Nisbet, editors, *Contemporary Social Problems* (New York: Harcourt, Brace and World, Inc., 1961), pp. 697–737; and Talcott Parsons, *The Social System* (New York: The Free Press of Glencoe, 1951), pp. 249–325.

5. Howard Brotz similarly identifies the question of what phenomena are "functional" or "dysfunctional" as a political one in "Functionalism and Dynamic Analysis," *European Journal of Sociology*, II (1961), 170–179.

deviance as the failure to obey group rules. Once we have described the rules a group enforces on its members, we can say with some precision whether or not a person has violated them and is thus, on this view, deviant.

This view is closest to my own, but it fails to give sufficient weight to the ambiguities that arise in deciding which rules are to be taken as the yardstick against which behavior is measured and judged deviant. A society has many groups, each with its own set of rules, and people belong to many groups simultaneously. A person may break the rules of one group by the very act of abiding by the rules of another group. Is he, then, deviant? Proponents of this definition may object that while ambiguity may arise with respect to the rules peculiar to one or another group in society, there are some rules that are very generally agreed to by everyone, in which case the difficulty does not arise. This, of course, is a question of fact, to be settled by empirical research. I doubt there are many such areas of consensus and think it wiser to use a definition that allows us to deal with both ambiguous and unambiguous situations.

Deviance and the Responses of Others

The sociological view I have just discussed defines deviance as the infraction of some agreed-upon rule. It then goes on to ask who breaks rules, and to search for the factors in their personalities and life situations that might account for the infractions. This assumes that those who have broken a rule constitute a homogeneous category, because they have committed the same deviant act.

Such an assumption seems to me to ignore the central fact about deviance: it is created by society. I do not mean this in the way it is ordinarily understood, in which the causes of deviance are located in the social situation of the deviant or in "social factors" which prompt his action. I mean, rather, that *social groups create deviance by making the rules whose infraction constitutes deviance*, and by applying those rules to particular people and labeling them as outsiders. From this point of view, deviance is *not* a quality of the act the person commits, but rather a consequence of the application by others of rules and sanctions to an "offender." The deviant is one to whom that label has successfully been applied; deviant behavior is behavior that people so label.[6]

Since deviance is, among other things, a consequence of the responses of others to a person's act, students of deviance cannot assume that they are dealing with a homogeneous category when they study people who have been labeled deviant. That is, they cannot assume that these people have actually committed a deviant act or broken some rule, because the process of labeling may not be infallible; some people may be labeled deviant who in fact have not broken a rule. Furthermore, they cannot assume that the category of those labeled deviant will contain all those who actually have broken a rule, for many offenders may escape apprehension and thus fail to be included in the population of "deviants" they study. Insofar as the category lacks homogeneity and fails to include all the cases that belong in it, one cannot reasonably expect to find common factors of personality or life situation that will account for the supposed deviance.

What, then, do people who have been labeled deviant have

6. The most important earlier statements of this view can be found in Frank Tannenbaum, *Crime and the Community* (New York: McGraw-Hill Book Co., Inc., 1951), and E. M. Lemert, *Social Pathology* (New York: McGraw-Hill Book Co., Inc., 1951). A recent article stating a position very similar to mine is John Kitsuse, "Societal Reaction to Deviance: Problems of Theory and Method," *Social Problems*, 9 (Winter, 1962), 247–256.

in common? At the least, they share the label and the experience of being labeled as outsiders. I will begin my analysis with this basic similarity and view deviance as the product of a transaction that takes place between some social group and one who is viewed by that group as a rule-breaker. I will be less concerned with the personal and social characteristics of deviants than with the process by which they come to be thought of as outsiders and their reactions to that judgment.

Malinowski discovered the usefulness of this view for understanding the nature of deviance many years ago, in his study of the Trobriand Islands:

> One day an outbreak of wailing and a great commotion told me that a death had occurred somewhere in the neighborhood. I was informed that Kima'i, a young lad of my acquaintance, of sixteen or so, had fallen from a coco-nut palm and killed himself. . . . I found that another youth had been severely wounded by some mysterious coincidence. And at the funeral there was obviously a general feeling of hostility between the village where the boy died and that into which his body was carried for burial.
>
> Only much later was I able to discover the real meaning of these events. The boy had committed suicide. The truth was that he had broken the rules of exogamy, the partner in his crime being his maternal cousin, the daughter of his mother's sister. This had been known and generally disapproved of but nothing was done until the girl's discarded lover, who had wanted to marry her and who felt personally injured, took the initiative. This rival threatened first to use black magic against the guilty youth, but this had not much effect. Then one evening he insulted the culprit in public—accusing him in the hearing of the whole community of incest and hurling at him certain expressions intolerable to a native.
>
> For this there was only one remedy; only one means of escape remained to the unfortunate youth. Next morning he put on festive attire and ornamentation, climbed a coco-nut palm and addressed the community, speaking from among the palm leaves and bidding them farewell. He explained the reasons for his

desperate deed and also launched forth a veiled accusation against the man who had driven him to his death, upon which it became the duty of his clansmen to avenge him. Then he wailed aloud, as is the custom, jumped from a palm some sixty feet high and was killed on the spot. There followed a fight within the village in which the rival was wounded; and the quarrel was repeated during the funeral. . . .

If you were to inquire into the matter among the Trobrianders, you would find . . . that the natives show horror at the idea of violating the rules of exogamy and that they believe that sores, disease and even death might follow clan incest. This is the ideal of native law, and in moral matters it is easy and pleasant strictly to adhere to the ideal—when judging the conduct of others or expressing an opinion about conduct in general.

When it comes to the application of morality and ideals to real life, however, things take on a different complexion. In the case described it was obvious that the facts would not tally with the ideal of conduct. Public opinion was neither outraged by the knowledge of the crime to any extent, nor did it react directly—it had to be mobilized by a public statement of the crime and by insults being hurled at the culprit by an interested party. Even then he had to carry out the punishment himself. . . . Probing further into the matter and collecting concrete information, I found that the breach of exogamy—as regards intercourse and not marriage—is by no means a rare occurrence, and public opinion is lenient, though decidedly hypocritical. If the affair is carried on *sub rosa* with a certain amount of decorum, and if no one in particular stirs up trouble—"public opinion" will gossip, but not demand any harsh punishment. If, on the contrary, scandal breaks out—everyone turns against the guilty pair and by ostracism and insults one or the other may be driven to suicide.[7]

Whether an act is deviant, then, depends on how other people react to it. You can commit clan incest and suffer from no more than gossip as long as no one makes a public accusa-

7. Bronislaw Malinowski, *Crime and Custom in Savage Society* (New York: Humanities Press, 1926), pp. 77-80. Reprinted by permission of Humanities Press and Routledge & Kegan Paul, Ltd.

tion; but you will be driven to your death if the accusation is made. The point is that the response of other people has to be regarded as problematic. Just because one has committed an infraction of a rule does not mean that others will respond as though this had happened. (Conversely, just because one has not violated a rule does not mean that he may not be treated, in some circumstances, as though he had.)

The degree to which other people will respond to a given act as deviant varies greatly. Several kinds of variation seem worth noting. First of all, there is variation over time. A person believed to have committed a given "deviant" act may at one time be responded to much more leniently than he would be at some other time. The occurrence of "drives" against various kinds of deviance illustrates this clearly. At various times, enforcement officials may decide to make an all-out attack on some particular kind of deviance, such as gambling, drug addiction, or homosexuality. It is obviously much more dangerous to engage in one of these activities when a drive is on than at any other time. (In a very interesting study of crime news in Colorado newspapers, Davis found that the amount of crime reported in Colorado newspapers showed very little association with actual changes in the amount of crime taking place in Colorado. And, further, that peoples' estimate of how much increase there had been in crime in Colorado was associated with the increase in the amount of crime news but not with any increase in the amount of crime.) [8]

The degree to which an act will be treated as deviant depends also on who commits the act and who feels he has been harmed by it. Rules tend to be applied more to some persons than others. Studies of juvenile delinquency make the point clearly. Boys from middle-class areas do not get as far in the

8. F. James Davis, "Crime News in Colorado Newspapers," *American Journal of Sociology*, LVII (January, 1952), 325–330.

legal process when they are apprehended as do boys from slum areas. The middle-class boy is less likely, when picked up by the police, to be taken to the station; less likely when taken to the station to be booked; and it is extremely unlikely that he will be convicted and sentenced.[9] This variation occurs even though the original infraction of the rule is the same in the two cases. Similarly, the law is differentially applied to Negroes and whites. It is well known that a Negro believed to have attacked a white woman is much more likely to be punished than a white man who commits the same offense; it is only slightly less well known that a Negro who murders another Negro is much less likely to be punished than a white man who commits murder.[10] This, of course, is one of the main points of Sutherland's analysis of white-collar crime: crimes committed by corporations are almost always prosecuted as civil cases, but the same crime committed by an individual is ordinarily treated as a criminal offense.[11]

Some rules are enforced only when they result in certain consequences. The unmarried mother furnishes a clear example. Vincent [12] points out that illicit sexual relations seldom result in severe punishment or social censure for the offenders. If, however, a girl becomes pregnant as a result of such activities the reaction of others is likely to be severe. (The illicit pregnancy is also an interesting example of the differential enforcement of rules on different categories of people. Vincent notes that unmarried fathers escape the severe censure visited on the mother.)

9. See Albert K. Cohen and James F. Short, Jr., "Juvenile Delinquency," in Merton and Nisbet, *op. cit.*, p. 87.

10. See Harold Garfinkel, "Research Notes on Inter- and Intra-Racial Homicides," *Social Forces*, 27 (May, 1949), 369–381.

11. Edwin H. Sutherland, "White Collar Criminality," *American Sociological Review*, V (February, 1940), 1–12.

12. Clark Vincent, *Unmarried Mothers* (New York: The Free Press of Glencoe, 1961), pp. 3–5.

Why repeat these commonplace observations? Because, taken together, they support the proposition that deviance is not a simple quality, present in some kinds of behavior and absent in others. Rather, it is the product of a process which involves responses of other people to the behavior. The same behavior may be an infraction of the rules at one time and not at another; may be an infraction when committed by one person, but not when committed by another; some rules are broken with impunity, others are not. In short, whether a given act is deviant or not depends in part on the nature of the act (that is, whether or not it violates some rule) and in part on what other people do about it.

Some people may object that this is merely a terminological quibble, that one can, after all, define terms any way he wants to and that if some people want to speak of rule-breaking behavior as deviant without reference to the reactions of others they are free to do so. This, of course, is true. Yet it might be worthwhile to refer to such behavior as *rule-breaking behavior* and reserve the term *deviant* for those labeled as deviant by some segment of society. I do not insist that this usage be followed. But it should be clear that insofar as a scientist uses "deviant" to refer to any rule-breaking behavior and takes as his subject of study only those who have been *labeled* deviant, he will be hampered by the disparities between the two categories.

If we take as the object of our attention behavior which comes to be labeled as deviant, we must recognize that we cannot know whether a given act will be categorized as deviant until the response of others has occurred. Deviance is not a quality that lies in behavior itself, but in the interaction between the person who commits an act and those who respond to it.

Whose Rules?

I have been using the term "outsiders" to refer to those people who are judged by others to be deviant and thus to stand outside the circle of "normal" members of the group. But the term contains a second meaning, whose analysis leads to another important set of sociological problems: "outsiders," from the point of view of the person who is labeled deviant, may be the people who make the rules he had been found guilty of breaking.

Social rules are the creation of specific social groups. Modern societies are not simple organizations in which everyone agrees on what the rules are and how they are to be applied in specific situations. They are, instead, highly differentiated along social class lines, ethnic lines, occupational lines, and cultural lines. These groups need not and, in fact, often do not share the same rules. The problems they face in dealing with their environment, the history and traditions they carry with them, all lead to the evolution of different sets of rules. Insofar as the rules of various groups conflict and contradict one another, there will be disagreement about the kind of behavior that is proper in any given situation.

Italian immigrants who went on making wine for themselves and their friends during Prohibition were acting properly by Italian immigrant standards, but were breaking the law of their new country (as, of course, were many of their Old American neighbors). Medical patients who shop around for a doctor may, from the perspective of their own group, be doing what is necessary to protect their health by making sure they get what seems to them the best possible doctor; but, from the perspective of the physician, what they do is wrong because it breaks down the trust the patient ought to put in his physician. The lower-class delinquent who fights for his "turf" is only doing what he considers necessary and right, but teachers, social workers, and police see it differently.

While it may be argued that many or most rules are generally agreed to by all members of a society, empirical research on a given rule generally reveals variation in people's attitudes. Formal rules, enforced by some specially constituted group, may differ from those actually thought appropriate by most people.[13] Factions in a group may disagree on what I have called actual operating rules. Most important for the study of behavior ordinarily labeled deviant, the perspectives of the people who engage in the behavior are likely to be quite different from those of the people who condemn it. In this latter situation, a person may feel that he is being judged according to rules he has had no hand in making and does not accept, rules forced on him by outsiders.

To what extent and under what circumstances do people attempt to force their rules on others who do not subscribe to them? Let us distinguish two cases. In the first, only those who are actually members of the group have any interest in making and enforcing certain rules. If an orthodox Jew disobeys the laws of kashruth only other orthodox Jews will regard this as a transgression; Christians or nonorthodox Jews will not consider this deviance and would have no interest in interfering. In the second case, members of a group consider it important to their welfare that members of certain other groups obey certain rules. Thus, people consider it extremely important that those who practice the healing arts abide by certain rules; this is the reason the state licenses physicians,

13. Arnold M. Rose and Arthur E. Prell, "Does the Punishment Fit the Crime?—A Study in Social Valuation," *American Journal of Sociology*, LXI (November, 1955), 247–259.

nurses, and others, and forbids anyone who is not licensed to engage in healing activities.

To the extent that a group tries to impose its rules on other groups in the society, we are presented with a second question: Who can, in fact, force others to accept their rules and what are the causes of their success? This is, of course, a question of political and economic power. Later we will consider the political and economic process through which rules are created and enforced. Here it is enough to note that people are in fact always *forcing* their rules on others, applying them more or less against the will and without the consent of those others. By and large, for example, rules are made for young people by their elders. Though the youth of this country exert a powerful influence culturally—the mass media of communication are tailored to their interests, for instance —many important kinds of rules are made for our youth by adults. Rules regarding school attendance and sex behavior are not drawn up with regard to the problems of adolescence. Rather, adolescents find themselves surrounded by rules about these matters which have been made by older and more settled people. It is considered legitimate to do this, for youngsters are considered neither wise enough nor responsible enough to make proper rules for themselves.

In the same way, it is true in many respects that men make the rules for women in our society (though in America this is changing rapidly). Negroes find themselves subject to rules made for them by whites. The foreign-born and those otherwise ethnically peculiar often have their rules made for them by the Protestant Anglo-Saxon minority. The middle class makes rules the lower class must obey—in the schools, the courts, and elsewhere.

Differences in the ability to make rules and apply them to other people are essentially power differentials (either legal or extralegal). Those groups whose social position gives them weapons and power are best able to enforce their rules. Distinctions of age, sex, ethnicity, and class are all related to differences in power, which accounts for differences in the degree to which groups so distinguished can make rules for others.

In addition to recognizing that deviance is created by the responses of people to particular kinds of behavior, by the labeling of that behavior as deviant, we must also keep in mind that the rules created and maintained by such labeling are not universally agreed to. Instead, they are the object of conflict and disagreement, part of the political process of society.

2 *Kinds*
of Deviance

A SEQUENTIAL MODEL

IT is not my purpose here to argue that only acts which are regarded as deviant by others are "really" deviant. But it must be recognized that this is an important dimension, one which needs to be taken into account in any analysis of deviant behavior. By combining this dimension with another—whether or not an act conforms to a particular rule—we can construct the following set of categories for the discrimination of different kinds of deviance.

Two of these types require very little explanation. *Conforming* behavior is simply that which obeys the rule and which others perceive as obeying the rule. At the other extreme, the *pure deviant* type of behavior is that which both disobeys the rule and is perceived as doing so.*

Types of Deviant Behavior

	Obedient Behavior	Rule-breaking Behavior
Perceived as deviant	Falsely accused	Pure deviant
Not perceived as deviant	Conforming	Secret deviant

The two other possibilities are of more interest. The *falsely accused* situation is what criminals often refer to as a "bum rap." The person is seen by others as having committed an improper action, although in fact he has not done so. False accusations undoubtedly occur even in courts of law, where the person is protected by rules of due process and evidence. They probably occur much more frequently in nonlegal settings where procedural safeguards are not available.

An even more interesting kind of case is found at the other extreme of *secret deviance.* Here an improper act is committed, yet no one notices it or reacts to it as a violation of the rules. As in the case of false accusation, no one really knows how much of this phenomenon exists, but I am convinced the amount is very sizable, much more so than we are apt to think. One brief observation convinces me this is the case. Most people probably think of fetishism (and sado-masochistic fetishism in particular) as a rare and exotic perversion. I had occasion several years ago, however, to examine the catalog of a dealer in pornographic pictures designed exclusively for devotees of this specialty. The catalog contained no pictures

* It should be remembered that this classification must always be used from the perspective of a given set of rules; it does not take into account the complexities, already discussed, that appear when there is more than one set of rules available for use by the same people in defining the same act. Furthermore, the classification has reference to types of behavior rather than types of people, to acts rather than personalities. The same person's behavior can obviously be conforming in some activities, deviant in others.

of nudes, no pictures of any version of the sex act. Instead, it contained page after page of pictures of girls in straitjackets, girls wearing boots with six-inch heels, girls holding whips, girls in handcuffs, and girls spanking one another. Each page served as a sample of as many as 120 pictures stocked by the dealer. A quick calculation revealed that the catalog advertised for immediate sale somewhere between fifteen and twenty thousand different photographs. The catalog itself was expensively printed and this fact, taken together with the number of photographs for sale, indicated clearly that the dealer did a land-office business and had a very sizable clientele. Yet one does not run across sado-masochistic fetishists every day. Obviously, they are able to keep the fact of their perversion secret ("All orders mailed in a plain envelope").[1]

Similar observations have been made by students of homosexuality, who note that many homosexuals are able to keep their deviance secret from their nondeviant associates. And many users of narcotic drugs, as we shall see later, are able to hide their addiction from the nonusers they associate with.

The four theoretical types of deviance, which we created by cross-classifying kinds of behavior and the responses they evoke, distinguish between phenomena that differ in important respects but are ordinarily considered to be similar. If we ignore the differences we may commit the fallacy of trying to explain several different kinds of things in the same way, and ignore the possibility that they may require different explanations. A boy who is innocently hanging around the fringes of a delinquent group may be arrested with them some night on suspicion. He will show up in the official statistics as a delinquent just as surely as those who have actually been involved in wrongdoing, and social scientists who try to de-

1. See also the discussion in James Jackson Kilpatrick, *The Smut Peddlers* (New York: Doubleday and Co., 1960), pp. 1–77.

velop theories to explain delinquency will attempt to account for his presence in the official records in the same way they try to account for the presence of the others.[2] But the cases are different; the same explanation will not do for both.

Simultaneous and
Sequential Models of Deviance

The discrimination of types of deviance may help us understand how deviant behavior originates. It will do so by enabling us to develop a sequential model of deviance, a model that allows for change through time. But before discussing the model itself, let us consider the differences between a sequential model and a simultaneous model in the development of individual behavior.

First of all, let us note that almost all research in deviance deals with the kind of question that arises from viewing it as pathological. That is, research attempts to discover the "etiology" of the "disease." It attempts to discover the causes of unwanted behavior.

This search is typically undertaken with the tools of multivariate analysis. The techniques and tools used in social research invariably contain a theoretical as well as a methodological commitment, and such is the case here. Multivariate analysis assumes (even though its users may in fact know better) that all the factors which operate to produce the phenomenon under study operate simultaneously. It seeks to discover which variable or what combination of variables will best "predict" the behavior one is studying. Thus, a study of juvenile delinquency may attempt to discover whether it is

2. I have profited greatly from reading an unpublished paper by John Kitsuse on the use of official statistics in research on deviance.

22

the intelligence quotient, the area in which a child lives, whether or not he comes from a broken home, or a combination of these factors that accounts for his being delinquent.

But, in fact, all causes do not operate at the same time, and we need a model which takes into account the fact that patterns of behavior *develop* in orderly sequence. In accounting for an individual's use of marihuana, as we shall see later, we must deal with a sequence of steps, of changes in the individual's behavior and perspectives, in order to understand the phenomenon. Each step requires explanation, and what may operate as a cause at one step in the sequence may be of negligible importance at another step. We need, for example, one kind of explanation of how a person comes to be in a situation where marihuana is easily available to him, and another kind of explanation of why, given the fact of its availability, he is willing to experiment with it in the first place. And we need still another explanation of why, having experimented with it, he continues to use it. In a sense, each explanation constitutes a necessary cause of the behavior. That is, no one could become a confirmed marihuana user without going through each step. He must have the drug available, experiment with it, and continue to use it. The explanation of each step is thus part of the explanation of the resulting behavior.

Yet the variables which account for each step may not, taken separately, distinguish between users and nonusers. The variable which disposes a person to take a particular step may not operate because he has not yet reached the stage in the process where it is possible to take that step. Let us suppose, for example, that one of the steps in the formation of an habitual pattern of drug use—willingness to experiment with use of the drug—is really the result of a variable of personality or personal orientation such as alienation from conventional norms. The variable of personal alienation, however, will only

23

produce drug use in people who are in a position to experiment because they participate in groups in which drugs are available; alienated people who do not have drugs available to them cannot begin experimentation and thus cannot become users, no matter how alienated they are. Thus alienation might be a necessary cause of drug use, but distinguish between users and nonusers only at a particular stage in the process.

A useful conception in developing sequential models of various kinds of deviant behavior is that of *career*.[3] Originally developed in studies of occupations, the concept refers to the sequence of movements from one position to another in an occupational system made by any individual who works in that system. Furthermore, it includes the notion of "career contingency," those factors on which mobility from one position to another depends. Career contingencies include both objective facts of social structure and changes in the perspectives, motivations, and desires of the individual. Ordinarily, in the study of occupations, we use the concept to distinguish between those who have a "successful" career (in whatever terms success is defined within the occupation) and those who do not. It can also be used to distinguish several varieties of career outcomes, ignoring the question of "success."

The model can easily be transformed for use in the study of deviant careers. In so transforming it, we should not confine our interest to those who follow a career that leads them into ever-increasing deviance, to those who ultimately take on an extremely deviant identity and way of life. We should also consider those who have a more fleeting contact with deviance,

3. See Everett C. Hughes, *Men and Their Work* (New York: The Free Press of Glencoe, 1958), pp. 56–67, 102–115, and 157–168; Oswald Hall, "The Stages of the Medical Career," *American Journal of Sociology*, LIII (March, 1948), 243–253; and Howard S. Becker and Anselm L. Strauss, "Careers, Personality, and Adult Socialization," *American Journal of Sociology*, LXII (November, 1956), 253–263.

whose careers lead them away from it into conventional ways of life. Thus, for example, studies of delinquents who fail to become adult criminals might teach us even more than studies of delinquents who progress in crime.

In the rest of this chapter I will consider the possibilities inherent in the career approach to deviance. Then I will turn to a study of a particular kind of deviance: the use of marihuana.

Deviant Careers

The first step in most deviant careers is the commission of a nonconforming act, an act that breaks some particular set of rules. How are we to account for the first step?

People usually think of deviant acts as motivated. They believe that the person who commits a deviant act, even for the first time (and perhaps especially for the first time), does so purposely. His purpose may or may not be entirely conscious, but there is a motive force behind it. We shall turn to the consideration of cases of intentional nonconformity in a moment, but first I must point out that many nonconforming acts are committed by people who have no intention of doing so; these clearly require a different explanation.

Unintended acts of deviance can probably be accounted for relatively simply. They imply an ignorance of the existence of the rule, or of the fact that it was applicable in this case, or to this particular person. But it is necessary to account for the lack of awareness. How does it happen that the person does not know his act is improper? Persons deeply involved in a particular subculture (such as a religious or ethnic subculture) may simply be unaware that everyone does not act "that way" and thereby commit an impropriety. There may,

25

in fact, be structured areas of ignorance of particular rules. Mary Haas has pointed out the interesting case of interlingual word taboos.[4] Words which are perfectly proper in one language have a "dirty" meaning in another. So the person, innocently using a word common in his own language, finds that he has shocked and horrified his listeners who come from a different culture.

In analyzing cases of intended nonconformity, people usually ask about motivation: why does the person want to do the deviant thing he does? The question assumes that the basic difference between deviants and those who conform lies in the character of their motivation. Many theories have been propounded to explain why some people have deviant motivations and others do not. Psychological theories find the cause of deviant motivations and acts in the individual's early experiences, which produce unconscious needs that must be satisfied if the individual is to maintain his equilibrium. Sociological theories look for socially structured sources of "strain" in the society, social positions which have conflicting demands placed upon them such that the individual seeks an illegitimate way of solving the problems his position presents him with. (Merton's famous theory of anomie fits into this category.)[5]

But the assumption on which these approaches are based may be entirely false. There is no reason to assume that only those who finally commit a deviant act actually have the impulse to do so. It is much more likely that most people experience deviant impulses frequently. At least in fantasy, people are much more deviant than they appear. Instead of asking why deviants want to do things that are disapproved

4. Mary R. Haas, "Interlingual Word Taboos," *American Anthropologist*, 53 (July–September, 1951), 338–344.
5. Robert K. Merton, *Social Theory and Social Structure* (New York: The Free Press of Glencoe, 1957), pp. 131–194.

of, we might better ask why conventional people do not follow through on the deviant impulses they have.

Something of an answer to this question may be found in the process of commitment through which the "normal" person becomes progressively involved in conventional institutions and behavior. In speaking of commitment,[6] I refer to the process through which several kinds of interests become bound up with carrying out certain lines of behavior to which they seem formally extraneous. What happens is that the individual, as a consequence of actions he has taken in the past or the operation of various institutional routines, finds he must adhere to certain lines of behavior, because many other activities than the one he is immediately engaged in will be adversely affected if he does not. The middle-class youth must not quit school, because his occupational future depends on receiving a certain amount of schooling. The conventional person must not indulge his interests in narcotics, for example, because much more than the pursuit of immediate pleasure is involved; his job, his family, and his reputation in his neighborhood may seem to him to depend on his continuing to avoid temptation.

In fact, the normal development of people in our society (and probably in any society) can be seen as a series of progressively increasing commitments to conventional norms and institutions. The "normal" person, when he discovers a deviant impulse in himself, is able to check that impulse by thinking of the manifold consequences acting on it would produce for him. He has staked too much on continuing to be normal

6. I have dealt with this concept at greater length in "Notes on the Concept of Commitment," *American Journal of Sociology*, LXVI (July, 1960), 32–40. See also Erving Goffman, *Encounters: Two Studies in the Sociology of Interaction* (Indianapolis: The Bobbs-Merrill Co., Inc., 1961), pp. 88–110; and Gregory P. Stone, "Clothing and Social Relations: A Study of Appearance in the Context of Community Life" (unpublished Ph.D. dissertation, Department of Sociology, University of Chicago, 1959).

to allow himself to be swayed by unconventional impulses.

This suggests that in looking at cases of intended nonconformity we must ask how the person manages to avoid the impact of conventional commitments. He may do so in one of two ways. First of all, in the course of growing up the person may somehow have avoided entangling alliances with conventional society. He may, thus, be free to follow his impulses. The person who does not have a reputation to maintain or a conventional job he must keep may follow his impulses. He has nothing staked on continuing to appear conventional.

However, most people remain sensitive to conventional codes of conduct and must deal with their sensitivities in order to engage in a deviant act for the first time. Sykes and Matza have suggested that delinquents actually feel strong impulses to be law-abiding, and deal with them by techniques of neutralization: "justifications for deviance that are seen as valid by the delinquent but not by the legal system or society at large." They distinguish a number of techniques for neutralizing the force of law-abiding values.

In so far as the delinquent can define himself as lacking responsibility for his deviant actions, the disapproval of self or others is sharply reduced in effectiveness as a restraining influence. . . . The delinquent approaches a "billiard ball" conception of himself in which he sees himself as helplessly propelled into new situations. . . . By learning to view himself as more acted upon than acting, the delinquent prepares the way for deviance from the dominant normative system without the necessity of a frontal assault on the norms themselves. . . .

A second major technique of neutralization centers on the injury or harm involved in the delinquent act. . . . For the delinquent . . . wrongfulness may turn on the question of whether or not anyone has clearly been hurt by his deviance, and this matter is open to a variety of interpretations. . . . Auto theft may be viewed as "borrowing," and gang fighting may be seen as a private quarrel, an agreed upon duel between two willing parties, and thus of no concern to the community at large. . . .

The moral indignation of self and others may be neutralized by an insistence that the injury is not wrong in light of the circumstances. The injury, it may be claimed, is not really an injury; rather, it is a form of rightful retaliation or punishment. . . . Assaults on homosexuals or suspected homosexuals, attacks on members of minority groups who are said to have gotten "out of place," vandalism as revenge on an unfair teacher or school official, thefts from a "crooked" store owner—all may be hurts inflicted on a transgressor, in the eyes of the delinquent. . . .

A fourth technique of neutralization would appear to involve a condemnation of the condemners. . . . His condemners, he may claim, are hypocrites, deviants in disguise, or impelled by personal spite. . . . By attacking others, the wrongfulness of his own behavior is more easily repressed or lost to view. . . .

Internal and external social controls may be neutralized by sacrificing the demands of the larger society for the demands of the smaller social groups to which the delinquent belongs such as the sibling pair, the gang, or the friendship clique. . . . The most important point is that deviation from certain norms may occur not because the norms are rejected but because other norms, held to be more pressing or involving a higher loyalty, are accorded precedence.[7]

In some cases a nonconforming act may appear necessary or expedient to a person otherwise law-abiding. Undertaken in pursuit of legitimate interests, the deviant act becomes, if not quite proper, at least not quite improper. In a novel dealing with a young Italian-American doctor we find a good example.[8] The young man, just out of medical school, would

7 Gresham M. Sykes and David Matza, "Techniques of Neutralization: A Theory of Delinquency," *American Sociological Review*, 22 (December, 1957), 667–669.

8. Guido D'Agostino, *Olives on the Apple Tree* (New York: Doubleday, Doran, 1940). I am grateful to Everett C. Hughes for calling this novel to my attention.

like to have a practice that is not built on the fact of his being Italian. But, being Italian, he finds it difficult to gain acceptance from the Yankee practitioners of his community. One day he is suddenly asked by one of the biggest surgeons to handle a case for him and thinks that he is finally being admitted to the referral system of the better doctors in town. But when the patient arrives at his office, he finds the case is an illegal abortion. Mistakenly seeing the referral as the first step in a regular relationship with the surgeon, he performs the operation. This act, although improper, is thought necessary to building his career.

But we are not so much interested in the person who commits a deviant act once as in the person who sustains a pattern of deviance over a long period of time, who makes of deviance a way of life, who organizes his identity around a pattern of deviant behavior. It is not the casual experimenters with homosexuality (who turned up in such surprisingly large numbers in the Kinsey Report) that we want to find out about, but the man who follows a pattern of homosexual activity throughout his adult life.

One of the mechanisms that lead from casual experimentation to a more sustained pattern of deviant activity is the development of deviant motives and interests. We shall examine this process in detail later, when we consider the career of the marihuana user. Here it is sufficient to say that many kinds of deviant activity spring from motives which are socially learned. Before engaging in the activity on a more or less regular basis, the person has no notion of the pleasures to be derived from it; he learns these in the course of interaction with more experienced deviants. He learns to be aware of new kinds of experiences and to think of them as pleasurable. What may well have been a random impulse to try something new becomes a settled taste for something already known and experienced. The vocabularies in which deviant motivations are phrased reveal that their users acquire them in interaction with other deviants. The individual *learns*, in short, to participate in a subculture organized around the particular deviant activity.

Deviant motivations have a social character even when most of the activity is carried on in a private, secret, and solitary fashion. In such cases, various media of communication may take the place of face-to-face interaction in inducting the individual into the culture. The pornographic pictures I mentioned earlier were described to prospective buyers in a stylized language. Ordinary words were used in a technical shorthand designed to whet specific tastes. The word "bondage," for instance, was used repeatedly to refer to pictures of women restrained in handcuffs or straitjackets. One does not acquire a taste for "bondage photos" without having learned what they are and how they may be enjoyed.

One of the most crucial steps in the process of building a stable pattern of deviant behavior is likely to be the experience of being caught and publicly labeled as a deviant. Whether a person takes this step or not depends not so much on what he does as on what other people do, on whether or not they enforce the rule he has violated. Although I will consider the circumstances under which enforcement takes place in some detail later, two notes are in order here. First of all, even though no one else discovers the nonconformity or enforces the rules against it, the individual who has committed the impropriety may himself act as enforcer. He may brand himself as deviant because of what he has done and punish himself in one way or another for his behavior. This is not always or necessarily the case, but may occur. Second, there may be cases like those described by psychoanalysts in which the individual really wants to get caught and perpetrates his deviant act in such a way that it is almost sure he will be.

In any case, being caught and branded as deviant has

important consequences for one's further social participation and self-image. The most important consequence is a drastic change in the individual's public identity. Committing the improper act and being publicly caught at it place him in a new status. He has been revealed as a different kind of person from the kind he was supposed to be. He is labeled a "fairy," "dope fiend," "nut" or "lunatic," and treated accordingly.

In analyzing the consequences of assuming a deviant identity let us make use of Hughes' distinction between master and auxiliary status traits.[9] Hughes notes that most statuses have one key trait which serves to distinguish those who belong from those who do not. Thus the doctor, whatever else he may be, is a person who has a certificate stating that he has fulfilled certain requirements and is licensed to practice medicine; this is the master trait. As Hughes points out, in our society a doctor is also informally expected to have a number of auxiliary traits: most people expect him to be upper middle class, white, male, and Protestant. When he is not there is a sense that he has in some way failed to fill the bill. Similarly, though skin color is the master status trait determining who is Negro and who is white, Negroes are informally expected to have certain status traits and not to have others; people are surprised and find it anomalous if a Negro turns out to be a doctor or a college professor. People often have the master status trait but lack some of the auxiliary, informally expected characteristics; for example, one may be a doctor but be female or Negro.

Hughes deals with this phenomenon in regard to statuses that are well thought of, desired and desirable (noting that one may have the formal qualifications for entry into a status but be denied full entry because of lack of the proper auxiliary

9. Everett C. Hughes, "Dilemmas and Contradictions of Status," *American Journal of Sociology*, L (March, 1945), 353-359.

traits), but the same process occurs in the case of deviant statuses. Possession of one deviant trait may have a generalized symbolic value, so that people automatically assume that its bearer possesses other undesirable traits allegedly associated with it.

To be labeled a criminal one need only commit a single criminal offense, and this is all the term formally refers to. Yet the word carries a number of connotations specifying auxiliary traits characteristic of anyone bearing the label. A man who has been convicted of housebreaking and thereby labeled criminal is presumed to be a person likely to break into other houses; the police, in rounding up known offenders for investigation after a crime has been committed, operate on this premise. Further, he is considered likely to commit other kinds of crimes as well, because he has shown himself to be a person without "respect for the law." Thus, apprehension for one deviant act exposes a person to the likelihood that he will be regarded as deviant or undesirable in other respects.

There is one other element in Hughes' analysis we can borrow with profit: the distinction between master and subordinate statuses.[10] Some statuses, in our society as in others, override all other statuses and have a certain priority. Race is one of these. Membership in the Negro race, as socially defined, will override most other status considerations in most other situations; the fact that one is a physician or middle-class or female will not protect one from being treated as a Negro first and any of these other things second. The status of deviant (depending on the kind of deviance) is this kind of master status. One receives the status as a result of breaking a rule, and the identification proves to be more important than most others. One will be identified as a deviant first, before other identifications are made. The question is raised:

10. *Ibid.*

"What kind of person would break such an important rule?" And the answer is given: "One who is different from the rest of us, who cannot or will not act as a moral human being and therefore might break other important rules." The deviant identification becomes the controlling one.

Treating a person as though he were generally rather than specifically deviant produces a self-fulfilling prophecy. It sets in motion several mechanisms which conspire to shape the person in the image people have of him.[11] In the first place, one tends to be cut off, after being identified as deviant, from participation in more conventional groups, even though the specific consequences of the particular deviant activity might never of themselves have caused the isolation had there not also been the public knowledge and reaction to it. For example, being a homosexual may not affect one's ability to do office work, but to be known as a homosexual in an office may make it impossible to continue working there. Similarly, though the effects of opiate drugs may not impair one's working ability, to be known as an addict will probably lead to losing one's job. In such cases, the individual finds it difficult to conform to other rules which he had no intention or desire to break, and perforce finds himself deviant in these areas as well. The homosexual who is deprived of a "respectable" job by the discovery of his deviance may drift into unconventional, marginal occupations where it does not make so much difference. The drug addict finds himself forced into other illegitimate kinds of activity, such as robbery and theft, by the refusal of respectable employers to have him around.

When the deviant is caught, he is treated in accordance with the popular diagnosis of why he is that way, and the treatment itself may likewise produce increasing deviance.

11. See Marsh Ray, "The Cycle of Abstinence and Relapse Among Heroin Addicts," *Social Problems*, 9 (Fall, 1961), 132–140.

The drug addict, popularly considered to be a weak-willed individual who cannot forego the indecent pleasures afforded him by opiates, is treated repressively. He is forbidden to use drugs. Since he cannot get drugs legally, he must get them illegally. This forces the market underground and pushes the price of drugs up far beyond the current legitimate market price into a bracket that few can afford on an ordinary salary. Hence the treatment of the addict's deviance places him in a position where it will probably be necessary to resort to deceit and crime in order to support his habit.[12] The behavior is a consequence of the public reaction to the deviance rather than a consequence of the inherent qualities of the deviant act.

Put more generally, the point is that the treatment of deviants denies them the ordinary means of carrying on the routines of everyday life open to most people. Because of this denial, the deviant must of necessity develop illegitimate routines. The influence of public reaction may be direct, as in the instances considered above, or indirect, a consequence of the integrated character of the society in which the deviant lives.

Societies are integrated in the sense that social arrangements in one sphere of activity mesh with other activities in other spheres in particular ways and depend on the existence of these other arrangements. Certain kinds of work lives presuppose a certain kind of family life, as we shall see when we consider the case of the dance musician.

Many varieties of deviance create difficulties by failing to mesh with expectations in other areas of life. Homosexuality is a case in point. Homosexuals have difficulty in any area of social activity in which the assumption of normal sexual interests and propensities for marriage is made without question.

12. See *Drug Addiction: Crime or Disease?* Interim and Final Reports of the Joint Committee of the American Bar Association and the American Medical Association on Narcotic Drugs (Bloomington, Indiana: Indiana University Press, 1961).

In stable work organizations such as large business or industrial organizations there are often points at which the man who would be successful should marry; not to do so will make it difficult for him to do the things that are necessary for success in the organization and will thus thwart his ambitions. The necessity of marrying often creates difficult enough problems for the normal male, and places the homosexual in an almost impossible position. Similarly, in some male work groups where heterosexual prowess is required to retain esteem in the group, the homosexual has obvious difficulties. Failure to meet the expectations of others may force the individual to attempt deviant ways of achieving results automatic for the normal person.

Obviously, everyone caught in one deviant act and labeled a deviant does not move inevitably toward greater deviance in the way the preceding remarks might suggest. The prophecies do not always confirm themselves, the mechanisms do not always work. What factors tend to slow down or halt the movement toward increasing deviance? Under what circumstances do they come into play?

One suggestion as to how the person may be immunized against increasing deviance is found in a recent study of juvenile delinquents who "hustle" homosexuals.[13] These boys act as homosexual prostitutes to confirmed adult homosexuals. Yet they do not themselves become homosexual. Several things account for their failure to continue this kind of sexual deviancy. First, they are protected from police action by the fact that they are minors. If they are apprehended in a homosexual act, they will be treated as exploited children, although in fact they are the exploiters; the law makes the adult guilty. Second, they look on the homosexual acts they engage in simply

13. Albert J. Reiss, Jr., "The Social Integration of Queers and Peers," *Social Problems*, 9 (Fall, 1961), 102–120.

as a means of making money that is safer and quicker than robbery or similar activities. Third, the standards of their peer group, while permitting homosexual prostitution, allow only one kind of activity, and forbid them to get any special pleasure out of it or to permit any expressions of endearment from the adult with whom they have relations. Infractions of these rules, or other deviations from normal heterosexual activity, are severely punished by the boy's fellows.

Apprehension may not lead to increasing deviance if the situation in which the individual is apprehended for the first time occurs at a point where he can still choose between alternate lines of action. Faced, for the first time, with the possible ultimate and drastic consequences of what he is doing, he may decide that he does not want to take the deviant road, and turn back. If he makes the right choice, he will be welcomed back into the conventional community; but if he makes the wrong move, he will be rejected and start a cycle of increasing deviance.

Ray has shown, in the case of drug addicts, how difficult it can be to reverse a deviant cycle.[14] He points out that drug addicts frequently attempt to cure themselves and that the motivation underlying their attempts is an effort to show nonaddicts whose opinions they respect that they are really not as bad as they are thought to be. On breaking their habit successfully, they find, to their dismay, that people still treat them as though they were addicts (on the premise, apparently, of "once a junkie, always a junkie").

A final step in the career of a deviant is movement into an organized deviant group. When a person makes a definite move into an organized group—or when he realizes and accepts the fact that he has already done so—it has a powerful impact on his conception of himself. A drug addict once told

14. Ray, *op. cit.*

me that the moment she felt she was really "hooked" was when she realized she no longer had any friends who were not drug addicts.

Members of organized deviant groups of course have one thing in common: their deviance. It gives them a sense of common fate, of being in the same boat. From a sense of common fate, from having to face the same problems, grows a deviant subculture: a set of perspectives and understandings about what the world is like and how to deal with it, and a set of routine activities based on those perspectives. Membership in such a group solidifies a deviant identity.

Moving into an organized deviant group has several consequences for the career of the deviant. First of all, deviant groups tend, more than deviant individuals, to be pushed into rationalizing their position. At an extreme, they develop a very complicated historical, legal, and psychological justification for their deviant activity. The homosexual community is a good case. Magazines and books by homosexuals and for homosexuals include historical articles about famous homosexuals in history. They contain articles on the biology and physiology of sex, designed to show that homosexuality is a "normal" sexual response. They contain legal articles, pleading for civil liberties for homosexuals.[15] Taken together, this material provides a working philosophy for the active homosexual, explaining to him why he is the way he is, that other people have also been that way, and why it is all right for him to be that way.

Most deviant groups have a self-justifying rationale (or "ideology"), although seldom is it as well worked out as that of the homosexual. While such rationales do operate, as pointed out earlier, to neutralize the conventional attitudes

15. *One* and *The Mattachine Review* are magazines of this type that I have seen.

that deviants may still find in themselves toward their own behavior, they also perform another function. They furnish the individual with reasons that appear sound for continuing the line of activity he has begun. A person who quiets his own doubts by adopting the rationale moves into a more principled and consistent kind of deviance than was possible for him before adopting it.

The second thing that happens when one moves into a deviant group is that he learns how to carry on his deviant activity with a minimum of trouble. All the problems he faces in evading enforcement of the rule he is breaking have been faced before by others. Solutions have been worked out. Thus, the young thief meets older thieves who, more experienced than he is, explain to him how to get rid of stolen merchandise without running the risk of being caught. Every deviant group has a great stock of lore on such subjects and the new recruit learns it quickly.

Thus, the deviant who enters an organized and institutionalized deviant group is more likely than ever before to continue in his ways. He has learned, on the one hand, how to avoid trouble and, on the other hand, a rationale for continuing.

One further fact deserves mention. The rationales of deviant groups tend to contain a general repudiation of conventional moral rules, conventional institutions, and the entire conventional world. We will examine a deviant subculture later when we consider the case of the dance musician.

3 Becoming a Marihuana User

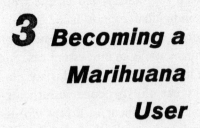

An unknown, but probably quite large, number of people in the United States use marihuana. They do this in spite of the fact that it is both illegal and disapproved.

The phenomenon of marihuana use has received much attention, particularly from psychiatrists and law enforcement officials. The research that has been done, as is often the case with research on behavior that is viewed as deviant, is mainly concerned with the question: why do they do it? Attempts to account for the use of marihuana lean heavily on the premise that the presence of any particular kind of behavior in an individual can best be explained as the result of some trait which predisposes or motivates him to engage in that behavior. In the case of marihuana use, this trait is usually identified as psychological, as a need for fantasy and escape from psychological problems the individual cannot face.[1]

I do not think such theories can adequately account for marihuana use. In fact, marihuana use is an interesting case for theories of deviance, because it illustrates the way deviant motives actually develop in the course of experience with the deviant activity. To put a complex argument in a few words: instead of the deviant motives leading to the deviant behavior, it is the other way around; the deviant behavior in time produces the deviant motivation. Vague impulses and desires—in this case, probably most frequently a curiosity about the kind of experience the drug will produce—are transformed into definite patterns of action through the social interpretation of a physical experience which is in itself ambiguous. Marihuana use is a function of the individual's conception of marihuana and of the uses to which it can be put, and this conception develops as the individual's experience with the drug increases.[2]

The research reported in this and the next chapter deals with the career of the marihuana user. In this chapter, we look at the development of the individual's immediate physical experience with marihuana. In the next, we consider the way he reacts to the various social controls that have grown up around use of the drug. What we are trying to understand here is the

1. See, as examples of this approach, the following: Eli Marcovitz and Henry J. Meyers, "The Marihuana Addict in the Army," *War Medicine*, VI (December, 1944), 382–391; Herbert S. Gaskill, "Marihuana, an Intoxicant," *American Journal of Psychiatry*, CII (September, 1945), 202–204; Sol Charen and Luis Perelman, "Personality Studies of Marihuana Addicts," *American Journal of Psychiatry*, CII (March, 1946), 674–682.

2. This theoretical point of view stems from George Herbert Mead's discussion of objects in *Mind, Self, and Society* (Chicago: University of Chicago Press, 1934), pp. 277–280.

sequence of changes in attitude and experience which lead to *the use of marihuana for pleasure.* This way of phrasing the problem requires a little explanation. Marihuana does not produce addiction, at least in the sense that alcohol and the opiate drugs do. The user experiences no withdrawal sickness and exhibits no ineradicable craving for the drug.[3] The most frequent pattern of use might be termed "recreational." The drug is used occasionally for the pleasure the user finds in it, a relatively casual kind of behavior in comparison with that connected with the use of addicting drugs. The report of the New York City Mayor's Committee on Marihuana emphasizes this point:

A person may be a confirmed smoker for a prolonged period, and give up the drug voluntarily without experiencing any craving for it or exhibiting withdrawal symptoms. He may, at some time later on, go back to its use. Others may remain infrequent users of the cigarette, taking one or two a week, or only when the "social setting" calls for participation. From time to time we had one of our investigators associate with a marihuana user. The investigator would bring up the subject of smoking. This would invariably lead to the suggestion that they obtain some marihuana cigarettes. They would seek a "tea-pad," and if it was closed the smoker and our investigator would calmly resume their previous activity, such as the discussion of life in general or the playing of pool. There were apparently no signs indicative of frustration in the smoker at not being able to gratify the desire for the drug. We consider this point highly significant since it is so contrary to the experience of users of other narcotics. A similar situation occurring in one addicted to the use of morphine, cocaine or heroin would result in a compulsive attitude on the part of the addict to obtain the drug. If unable to secure it, there would be obvious physical and mental manifestations of frustration. This may be considered presumptive evidence that there is no true

3. Cf. Rogers Adams, "Marihuana," *Bulletin of the New York Academy of Medicine,* XVIII (November, 1942), 705–730.

addiction in the medical sense associated with the use of mari-huana.[4]

In using the phrase "use for pleasure," I mean to emphasize the noncompulsive and casual character of the behavior. (I also mean to eliminate from consideration here those few cases in which marihuana is used for its prestige value only, as a symbol that one is a certain kind of person, with no pleasure at all being derived from its use.)

The research I am about to report was not so designed that it could constitute a crucial test of the theories that relate marihuana use to some psychological trait of the user. How-ever, it does show that psychological explanations are not in themselves sufficient to account for marihuana use and that they are, perhaps, not even necessary. Researchers attempting to prove such psychological theories have run into two great difficulties, never satisfactorily resolved, which the theory presented here avoids. In the first place, theories based on the existence of some predisposing psychological trait have diffi-culty in accounting for that group of users, who turn up in sizable numbers in every study,[5] who do not exhibit the trait or traits which are considered to cause the behavior. Second, psychological theories have difficulty in accounting for the great variability over time of a given individual's behavior with reference to the drug. The same person will at one time be unable to use the drug for pleasure, at a later stage be able and willing to do so, and still later again be unable to use it in this way. These changes, difficult to explain from a theory based on the user's needs for "escape" are readily understand-

4. The New York City Mayor's Committee on Marihuana, *The Mari-huana Problem in the City of New York* (Lancaster, Pennsylvania: Jacques Cattell Press, 1944), pp. 12–13.

5. Cf. Lawrence Kolb, "Marihuana," *Federal Probation*, II (July, 1938), 22–25; and Walter Bromberg, "Marihuana: A Psychiatric Study," *Journal of the American Medical Association*, CXIII (July 1, 1939), 11.

able as consequences of changes in his conception of the drug. Similarly, if we think of the marihuana user as someone who has learned to view marihuana as something that can give him pleasure, we have no difficulty in understanding the existence of psychologically "normal" users.

In doing the study, I used the method of analytic induction. I tried to arrive at a general statement of the sequence of changes in individual attitude and experience which always occurred when the individual became willing and able to use marihuana for pleasure, and never occurred or had not been permanently maintained when the person was unwilling to use marihuana for pleasure. The method requires that *every* case collected in the research substantiate the hypothesis. If one case is encountered which does not substantiate it, the researcher is required to change the hypothesis to fit the case which has proven his original idea wrong.[6]

To develop and test my hypothesis about the genesis of marihuana use for pleasure, I conducted fifty interviews with marihuana users. I had been a professional dance musician for some years when I conducted this study and my first interviews were with people I had met in the music business. I asked them to put me in contact with other users who would be willing to discuss their experiences with me. Colleagues working on a study of users of opiate drugs made a few interviews available to me which contained, in addition to material on opiate drugs, sufficient material on the use of marihuana to furnish a test of my hypothesis.[7] Although in the end half

6. The method is described in Alfred R. Lindesmith, *Opiate Addiction* (Bloomington, Indiana: Principia Press, 1947), chap. 1. There has been considerable discussion of this method in the literature. See, particularly, Ralph H. Turner, "The Quest for Universals in Sociological Research," *American Sociological Review*, 18 (December, 1953), 604–611, and the literature cited there.

7. I wish to thank Solomon Kobrin and Harold Finestone for making these interviews available to me.

of the fifty interviews were conducted with musicians, the other half covered a wide range of people, including laborers, machinists, and people in the professions. The sample is, of course, in no sense "random"; it would not be possible to draw a random sample, since no one knows the nature of the universe from which it would have to be drawn.

In interviewing users, I focused on the history of the person's experience with marihuana, seeking major changes in his attitude toward it and in his actual use of it, and the reasons for these changes. Where it was possible and appropriate, I used the jargon of the user himself.

The theory starts with the person who has arrived at the point of willingness to try marihuana. (I discuss how he got there in the next chapter.) He knows others use marihuana to "get high," but he does not know what this means in any concrete way. He is curious about the experience, ignorant of what it may turn out to be, and afraid it may be more than he has bargained for. The steps outlined below, if he undergoes them all and maintains the attitudes developed in them, leave him willing and able to use the drug for pleasure when the opportunity presents itself.

Learning the Technique

The novice does not ordinarily get high the first time he smokes marihuana, and several attempts are usually necessary to induce this state. One explanation of this may be that the drug is not smoked "properly," that is, in a way that insures sufficient dosage to produce real symptoms of intoxication. Most users agree that it cannot be smoked like tobacco if one is to get high:

Take in a lot of air, you know, and . . . I don't know how to describe it, you don't smoke it like a cigarette, you draw in a lot of air and get it deep down in your system and then keep it there. Keep it there as long as you can.

Without the use of some such technique [8] the drug will produce no effects, and the user will be unable to get high:

The trouble with people like that [who are not able to get high] is that they're just not smoking it right, that's all there is to it. Either they're not holding it down long enough, or they're getting too much air and not enough smoke, or the other way around or something like that. A lot of people just don't smoke it right, so naturally nothing's gonna happen.

If nothing happens, it is manifestly impossible for the user to develop a conception of the drug as an object which can be used for pleasure, and use will therefore not continue. The first step in the sequence of events that must occur if the person is to become a user is that he must learn to use the proper smoking technique so that his use of the drug will produce effects in terms of which his conception of it can change.

Such a change is, as might be expected, a result of the individual's participation in groups in which marihuana is used. In them the individual learns the proper way to smoke the drug. This may occur through direct teaching:

I was smoking like I did an ordinary cigarette. He said, "No, don't do it like that." He said, "Suck it, you know, draw in and hold it in your lungs till you . . . for a period of time."
I said, "Is there any limit of time to hold it?"
He said, "No, just till you feel that you want to let it out, let it out." So I did that three or four times.

8. A pharmacologist notes that this ritual is in fact an extremely efficient way of getting the drug into the blood stream. See R. P. Walton, *Marihuana: America's New Drug Problem* (Philadelphia: J. B. Lippincott, 1938). p. 48.

Many new users are ashamed to admit ignorance and, pretending to know already, must learn through the more indirect means of observation and imitation:

I came on like I had turned on [smoked marihuana] many times before, you know. I didn't want to seem like a punk to this cat. See, like I didn't know the first thing about it—how to smoke it, or what was going to happen, or what. I just watched him like a hawk—I didn't take my eyes off him for a second, because I wanted to do everything just as he did it. I watched how he held it, how he smoked it, and everything. Then when he gave it to me I just came on cool, as though I knew exactly what the score was. I held it like he did and took a poke just the way he did.

No one I interviewed continued marihuana use for pleasure without learning a technique that supplied sufficient dosage for the effects of the drug to appear. Only when this was learned was it possible for a conception of the drug as an object which could be used for pleasure to emerge. Without such a conception marihuana use was considered meaningless and did not continue.

Learning to Perceive the Effects

Even after he learns the proper smoking technique, the new user may not get high and thus not form a conception of the drug as something which can be used for pleasure. A remark made by a user suggested the reason for this difficulty in getting high and pointed to the next necessary step on the road to being a user:

As a matter of fact, I've seen a guy who was high out of his mind and didn't know it.
[How can that be, man?]
Well, it's pretty strange, I'll grant you that, but I've seen it.

This guy got on with me, claiming that he'd never got high, one of those guys, and he got completely stoned. And he kept insisting that he wasn't high. So I had to prove to him that he was.

What does this mean? It suggests that being high consists of two elements: the presence of symptoms caused by marihuana use and the recognition of these symptoms and their connection by the user with his use of the drug. It is not enough, that is, that the effects be present; alone, they do not automatically provide the experience of being high. The user must be able to point them out to himself and consciously connect them with having smoked marihuana before he can have this experience. Otherwise, no matter what actual effects are produced, he considers that the drug has had no effect on him: "I figured it either had no effect on me or other people were exaggerating its effect on them, you know. I thought it was probably psychological, see." Such persons believe the whole thing is an illusion and that the wish to be high leads the user to deceive himself into believing that something is happening when, in fact, nothing is. They do not continue marihuana use, feeling that "it does nothing" for them.

Typically, however, the novice has faith (developed from his observation of users who do get high) that the drug actually will produce some new experience and continues to experiment with it until it does. His failure to get high worries him, and he is likely to ask more experienced users or provoke comments from them about it. In such conversations he is made aware of specific details of his experience which he may not have noticed or may have noticed but failed to identify as symptoms of being high:

I didn't get high the first time. . . . I don't think I held it in long enough. I probably let it out, you know, you're a little afraid. The second time I wasn't sure, and he [smoking companion] told me, like I asked him for some of the symptoms or something,

49

how would I know, you know. . . . So he told me to sit on a stool. I sat on—I think I sat on a bar stool—and he said, "Let your feet hang," and then when I got down my feet were real cold, you know.

And I started feeling it, you know. That was the first time. And then about a week after that, sometime pretty close to it, I really got on. That was the first time I got on a big laughing kick, you know. Then I really knew I was on.

One symptom of being high is an intense hunger. In the next case the novice becomes aware of this and gets high for the first time:

They were just laughing the hell out of me because like I was eating so much. I just scoffed [ate] so much food, and they were just laughing at me, you know. Sometimes I'd be looking at them, you know, wondering why they're laughing, you know, not knowing what I was doing. [Well, did they tell you why they were laughing eventually?] Yeah, yeah, I come back, "Hey, man, what's happening?" Like, you know, like I'd ask, "What's happening?" and all of a sudden I feel weird, you know. "Man, you're on, you know. You're on pot [high on marihuana]." I said, "No, am I?" Like I don't know what's happening.

The learning may occur in more indirect ways:

I heard little remarks that were made by other people. Somebody said, "My legs are rubbery," and I can't remember all the remarks that were made because I was very attentively listening for all these cues for what I was supposed to feel like.

The novice, then, eager to have this feeling, picks up from other users some concrete referents of the term "high" and applies these notions to his own experience. The new concepts make it possible for him to locate these symptoms among his own sensations and to point out to himself a "something different" in his experience that he connects with drug use. It is only when he can do this that he is high. In the next case, the contrast between two successive experiences of a user makes clear the crucial importance of the awareness of the symptoms in being high and re-emphasizes the important role of interaction with other users in acquiring the concepts that make this awareness possible:

[Did you get high the first time you turned on?] Yeah, sure. Although, come to think of it, I guess I really didn't. I mean, like that first time it was more or less of a mild drunk. I was happy, I guess, you know what I mean. But I didn't really know I was high, you know what I mean. It was only after the second time I got high that I realized I was high the first time. Then I knew that something different was happening.

[How did you know that?] How did I know? If what happened to me that night would of happened to you, you would've known, believe me. We played the first tune for almost two hours—one tune! Imagine, man! We got on the stand and played this one tune, we started at nine o'clock. When we got finished I looked at my watch, it's a quarter to eleven. Almost two hours on one tune. And it didn't seem like anything.

I mean, you know, it does that to you. It's like you have much more time or something. Anyway, when I saw that, man, it was too much. I knew I must really be high or something if anything like that could happen. See, and then they explained to me that that's what it did to you, you had a different sense of time and everything. So I realized that that's what it was. I knew then. Like the first time, I probably felt that way, you know, but I didn't know what's happening.

It is only when the novice becomes able to get high in this sense that he will continue to use marihuana for pleasure. In every case in which use continued, the user had acquired the necessary concepts with which to express to himself the fact that he was experiencing new sensations caused by the drug. That is, for use to continue, it is necessary not only to use the drug so as to produce effects but also to learn to perceive these effects when they occur. In this way marihuana acquires meaning for the user as an object which can be used for pleasure

With increasing experience the user develops a greater appreciation of the drug's effects; he continues to learn to get high. He examines succeeding experiences closely, looking for new effects, making sure the old ones are still there. Out of this there grows a stable set of categories for experiencing the drug's effects whose presence enables the user to get high with ease.

Users, as they acquire this set of categories, become connoisseurs. Like experts in fine wines, they can specify where a particular plant was grown and what time of year it was harvested. Although it is usually not possible to know whether these attributions are correct, it is true that they distinguish between batches of marihuana, not only according to strength, but also with respect to the different kinds of symptoms produced.

The ability to perceive the drug's effects must be maintained if use is to continue; if it is lost, marihuana use ceases. Two kinds of evidence support this statement. First, people who become heavy users of alcohol, barbiturates, or opiates do not continue to smoke marihuana, largely because they lose the ability to distinguish between its effects and those of the other drugs.[9] They no longer know whether the marihuana gets them high. Second, in those few cases in which an individual uses marihuana in such quantities that he is always high, he is apt to feel the drug has no effect on him, since the essential element of a noticeable difference between feeling

9. "Smokers have repeatedly stated that the consumption of whiskey while smoking negates the potency of the drug. They find it very difficult to get 'high' while drinking whiskey and because of that smokers will not drink while using the 'weed.'" (New York City Mayor's Committee on Marihuana, *The Marihuana Problem in the City of New York, op. cit.*, p. 13.)

high and feeling normal is missing. In such a situation, use is likely to be given up completely, but temporarily, in order that the user may once again be able to perceive the difference.

Learning to Enjoy the Effects

One more step is necessary if the user who has now learned to get high is to continue use. He must learn to enjoy the effects he has just learned to experience. Marihuana-produced sensations are not automatically or necessarily pleasurable. The taste for such experience is a socially acquired one, not different in kind from acquired tastes for oysters or dry martinis. The user feels dizzy, thirsty; his scalp tingles; he misjudges time and distances. Are these things pleasurable? He isn't sure. If he is to continue marihuana use, he must decide that they are. Otherwise, getting high, while a real enough experience, will be an unpleasant one he would rather avoid.

The effects of the drug, when first perceived, may be physically unpleasant or at least ambiguous:

It started taking effect, and I didn't know what was happening, you know, what it was, and I was very sick. I walked around the room, walking around the room trying to get off, you know; it just scared me at first, you know. I wasn't used to that kind of feeling.

In addition, the novice's naïve interpretation of what is happening to him may further confuse and frighten him, particularly if he decides, as many do, that he is going insane:

I felt I was insane, you know. Everything people done to me just wigged me. I couldn't hold a conversation, and my mind would be wandering, and I was always thinking, oh, I don't know, weird things, like hearing music different. . . . I get the feeling that I can't talk to anyone. I'll goof completely.

Given these typically frightening and unpleasant first experiences, the beginner will not continue use unless he learns to redefine the sensations as pleasurable:

It was offered to me, and I tried it. I'll tell you one thing. I never did enjoy it at all. I mean it was just nothing that I could enjoy. [Well, did you get high when you turned on?] Oh, yeah, I got definite feelings from it. But I didn't enjoy them. I mean I got plenty of reactions, but they were mostly reactions of fear. [You were frightened?] Yes. I didn't enjoy it. I couldn't seem to relax with it, you know. If you can't relax with a thing, you can't enjoy it, I don't think.

In other cases the first experiences were also definitely unpleasant, but the person did become a marihuana user. This occurred, however, only after a later experience enabled him to redefine the sensations as pleasurable:

[This man's first experience was extremely unpleasant, involving distortion of spatial relationships and sounds, violent thirst, and panic produced by these symptoms.] After the first time I didn't turn on for about, I'd say, ten months to a year. . . . It wasn't a moral thing; it was because I'd gotten so frightened, bein' so high. An' I didn't want to go through that again, I mean, my reaction was, "Well, if this is what they call bein' high, I don't dig [like] it." . . . So I didn't turn on for a year almost, accounta that. . . .

Well, my friends started, an' consequently I started again. But I didn't have any more, I didn't have that same initial reaction, after I started turning on again.

[In interaction with his friends he became able to find pleasure in the effects of the drug and eventually became a regular user.]

In no case will use continue without a redefinition of the effects as enjoyable.

This redefinition occurs, typically, in interaction with more experienced users who, in a number of ways, teach the novice to find pleasure in this experience which is at first so frightening.[10] They may reassure him as to the temporary character of the unpleasant sensations and minimize their seriousness, at the same time calling attention to the more enjoyable aspects. An experienced user describes how he handles newcomers to marihuana use:

Well, they get pretty high sometimes. The average person isn't ready for that, and it is a little frightening to them sometimes. I mean, they've been high on lush [alcohol], and they get higher that way than they've ever been before, and they don't know what's happening to them. Because they think they're going to keep going up, up, up till they lose their minds or begin doing weird things or something. You have to like reassure them, explain to them that they're not really flipping or anything, that they're gonna be all right. You have to just talk them out of being afraid. Keep talking to them, reassuring, telling them it's all right. And come on with your own story, you know: "The same thing happened to me. You'll get to like that after awhile." Keep coming on like that; pretty soon you talk them out of being scared. And besides they see you doing it and nothing horrible is happening to you, so that gives them more confidence.

The more experienced user may also teach the novice to regulate the amount he smokes more carefully, so as to avoid any severely uncomfortable symptoms while retaining the pleasant ones. Finally, he teaches the new user that he can "get to like it after awhile." He teaches him to regard those ambiguous experiences formerly defined as unpleasant as enjoyable. The older user in the following incident is a person whose tastes have shifted in this way, and his remarks have the effect of helping others to make a similar redefinition:

A new user had her first experience of the effects of marihuana and became frightened and hysterical. She "felt like she was half in and half out of the room" and experienced a number of alarming physical symptoms. One of the more experienced

10. Charen and Perelman, *op. cit.*, p. 679.

users present said, "She's dragged because she's high like that. I'd give anything to get that high myself. I haven't been that high in years."

In short, what was once frightening and distasteful becomes, after a taste for it is built up, pleasant, desired, and sought after. Enjoyment is introduced by the favorable definition of the experience that one acquires from others. Without this, use will not continue, for marihuana will not be for the user an object he can use for pleasure.

In addition to being a necessary step in becoming a user, this represents an important condition for continued use. It is quite common for experienced users suddenly to have an unpleasant or frightening experience, which they cannot define as pleasurable, either because they have used a larger amount of marihuana than usual or because the marihuana they have used turns out to be of a higher quality than they expected. The user has sensations which go beyond any conception he has of what being high is and is in much the same situation as the novice, uncomfortable and frightened. He may blame it on an overdose and simply be more careful in the future. But he may make this the occasion for a rethinking of his attitude toward the drug and decide that it no longer can give him pleasure. When this occurs and is not followed by a redefinition of the drug as capable of producing pleasure, use will cease.

The likelihood of such a redefinition occurring depends on the degree of the individual's participation with other users. Where this participation is intensive, the individual is quickly talked out of his feeling against marihuana use. In the next case, on the other hand, the experience was very disturbing, and the aftermath of the incident cut the person's participation with other users to almost zero. Use stopped for three years and began again only when a combination of circumstances, important among which was a resumption of ties with users, made possible a redefinition of the nature of the drug:

It was too much, like I only made about four pokes, and I couldn't even get it out of my mouth, I was so high, and I got real flipped. In the basement, you know, I just couldn't stay in there anymore. My heart was pounding real hard, you know, and I was going out of my mind; I thought I was losing my mind completely. So I cut out of this basement, and this other guy, he's out of his mind, told me, "Don't, don't leave me, man. Stay here." And I couldn't.

I walked outside, and it was five below zero, and I thought I was dying, and I had my coat open; I was sweating, I was perspiring. My whole insides were all . . . , and I walked about two blocks away, and I fainted behind a bush. I don't know how long I laid there. I woke up, and I was feeling the worst, I can't describe it at all, so I made it to a bowling alley, man, and I was trying to act normal, I was trying to shoot pool, you know, trying to act real normal, and I couldn't lay and I couldn't stand up and I couldn't sit down, and I went up and laid down where some guys that spot pins lay down, and that didn't help me, and I went down to a doctor's office. I was going to go in there and tell the doctor to put me out of my misery . . . because my heart was pounding so hard, you know. . . . So then all week end I started flipping, seeing things there and going through hell, you know, all kinds of abnormal things. . . . I just quit for a long time then.

[He went to a doctor who defined the symptoms for him as those of a nervous breakdown caused by "nerves" and "worries." Although he was no longer using marihuana, he had some recurrences of the symptoms which led him to suspect that "it was all his nerves."] So I just stopped worrying, you know; so it was about thirty-six months later I started making it again. I'd just take a few pokes, you know. [He first resumed use in the company of the same user-friend with whom he had been involved in the original incident.]

A person, then, cannot begin to use marihuana for pleasure, or continue its use for pleasure, unless he learns to define its effects as enjoyable, unless it becomes and remains an object he conceives of as capable of producing pleasure.

In summary, an individual will be able to use marihuana for pleasure only when he goes through a process of learning to conceive of it as an object which can be used in this way. No one becomes a user without (1) learning to smoke the drug in a way which will produce real effects; (2) learning to recognize the effects and connect them with drug use (learning, in other words, to get high); and (3) learning to enjoy the sensations he perceives. In the course of this process he develops a disposition or motivation to use marihuana which was not and could not have been present when he began use, for it involves and depends on conceptions of the drug which could only grow out of the kind of actual experience detailed above. On completion of this process he is willing and able to use marihuana for pleasure.

He has learned, in short, to answer "Yes" to the question: "Is it fun?" The direction his further use of the drug takes depends on his being able to continue to answer "Yes" to this question and, in addition, on his being able to answer "Yes" to other questions which arise as he becomes aware of the implications of the fact that society disapproves of the practice: "Is it expedient?" "Is it moral?" Once he has acquired the ability to get enjoyment by using the drug, use will continue to be possible for him. Considerations of morality and expediency, occasioned by the reactions of society, may interfere and inhibit use, but use continues to be a possibility in terms of his conception of the drug. The act becomes impossible only when the ability to enjoy the experience of being high is lost, through a change in the user's conception of the drug occasioned by certain kinds of experience with it.

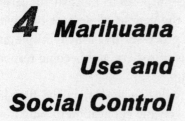

4 Marihuana Use and Social Control

LEARNING to enjoy marihuana is a necessary but not a sufficient condition for a person to develop a stable pattern of drug use. He has still to contend with the powerful forces of social control that make the act seem inexpedient, immoral, or both.

When deviant behavior occurs in a society—behavior which flouts its basic values and norms—one element in its coming into being is a breakdown in social controls which ordinarily operate to maintain the valued forms of behavior. In complex societies, the process can be quite complicated since breakdowns in social control are often the consequence of becoming a participant in a group whose own culture and social controls operate at cross-purposes to those of the larger society. Important factors in the genesis of deviant behavior, then, may be sought in the processes by which people are emancipated from the controls of society and become responsive to those of a smaller group.

Social controls affect individual behavior, in the first instance, through the use of power, the application of sanctions. Valued behavior is rewarded and negatively valued behavior is punished. Control would be difficult to maintain if enforcement were always needed, so that more subtle mechanisms performing the same function arise. Among these is the control of behavior achieved by affecting the conceptions persons have of the to-be-controlled activity, and of the possibility or feasibility of engaging in it. These conceptions arise in social situations in which they are communicated by persons regarded as reputable and validated in experience. Such situations may be so ordered that individuals come to conceive of the activity as distasteful, inexpedient, or immoral, and therefore do not engage in it.

This perspective invites us to analyze the genesis of deviant behavior in terms of events which render sanctions ineffective and experiences which shift conceptions so that the behavior becomes a conceivable possibility to the person. In this chapter I analyze this process in the instance of marihuana use. My basic question is: what is the sequence of events and experiences by which a person comes to be able to carry on the use of marihuana, in spite of the elaborate social controls functioning to prevent such behavior?

A number of potent forces operate to control the use of marihuana in this country. The act is illegal and punishable by severe penalties. Its illegality makes access to the drug difficult, placing immediate obstacles before anyone who wishes to use it. Actual use can be dangerous, for arrest and imprisonment are always possible consequences. In addition, if a user's family, friends, or employer discover that he uses marihuana, they may impute to him the auxiliary status traits ordinarily assumed to be associated with drug use. Believing him to be irresponsible and powerless to control his own behavior, perhaps even insane, they may punish him with various kinds of informal but highly effective sanctions, such as ostracism or withdrawal of affection. Finally, a set of traditional views has grown up, defining the practice as a violation of basic moral imperatives, as an act leading to loss of self-control, paralysis of the will, and eventual slavery to the drug. Such views are commonplace and are effective forces preventing marihuana use.

The career of the marihuana user may be divided into three stages, each representing a distinct shift in his relation to the social controls of the larger society and to those of the subculture in which marihuana use is found. The first stage is represented by the *beginner*, the person smoking marihuana for the first time; the second, by the *occasional user*, whose use is sporadic and dependent on chance factors; and the third, by the *regular user*, for whom use becomes a systematic, usually daily routine.

First let us consider the processes by which various kinds of social controls become progressively less effective as the user moves from level to level of use or, alternatively, the way controls prevent such movement by remaining effective. The major kinds of controls to be considered are: (a) control through limiting of supply and access to the drug; (b) control through the necessity of keeping nonusers from discovering that one is a user; (c) control through definition of the act as immoral. The rendering ineffective of these controls, at the levels and in the combinations to be described, may be taken as an essential condition for continued and increased marihuana use.

Supply

Marihuana use is limited, in the first instance, by laws making possession or sale of drug punishable by severe penalties. This confines its distribution to illicit sources not easily available to the ordinary person. In order for a person to begin marihuana use, he must begin participation in some group through which these sources of supply become available to him, ordinarily a group organized around values and activities opposing those of the larger conventional society.

In those unconventional circles in which marihuana is already used, it is apparently just a matter of time until a situation arises in which the newcomer is given a chance to smoke it:

I was with these guys that I knew from school, and one had some, so they went to get high and they just figured that I did too, they never asked me, so I didn't want to be no wallflower or nothin', so I didn't say nothin' and went out in the back of this place with them. They were doing up a couple of cigarettes.

In other groups marihuana is not immediately available, but participation in the group provides connections to others in which it is:

But the thing was, we didn't know where to get any. None of us knew where to get it or how to find out where to get it. Well, there was this one chick there . . . she had some spade [Negro] girl friends and she had turned on before with them. Maybe once or twice. But she knew a little more about it than any of the rest of us. So she got hold of some, through these spade friends, and one night she brought down a couple of sticks.

In either case, such participation provides the conditions under which marihuana becomes available for first use. It also provides the conditions for the next level of *occasional use*, in which the individual smokes marihuana sporadically and irregularly. When an individual has arrived through earlier experiences at a point where he is able to use marihuana for pleasure, use tends at first to be a function of availability. The person uses the drug when he is with others who have a supply; when this is not the case his use ceases. It tends therefore to fluctuate in terms of the conditions of availability created by his participation with other users; a musician at this stage of use said:

That's mostly when I get high, is when I play jobs. And I haven't played hardly at all lately . . . See, I'm married twelve years now, and I really haven't done much since then. I had to get a day job, you know, and I haven't been able to play much. I haven't had many gigs [jobs], so I really haven't turned on much, you see.

Like I say, the only time I really get on is if I'm working with some cats who do, then I will too. Like I say, I haven't been high for maybe six months. I haven't turned on in all that time. Then, since I come on this job, that's three weeks, I've been high every Friday and Saturday. That's the way it goes with me.

[This man was observed over a period of weeks to be completely dependent on other members of the orchestra in which he worked and on musicians who dropped into the tavern in which he was playing for any marihuana he used.]

If an occasional user begins to move on toward a more regularized and systematic mode of use, he can do it only by finding a more stable source of supply than more-or-less chance encounters with other users, and this means establish-

ing connections with persons who make a business of dealing
in narcotics. Although purchases in large quantities are necessary for regular use, they are not ordinarily made with that
intent; but, once made, they do render such use possible, as it
was not before. Such purchases tend to be made as the user
becomes more responsive to the controls of the drug-using
group:

I was running around with this whole crowd of people who
turned on then. And they were always turning me on, you know,
until it got embarrassing. I was really embarrassed that I never
had any, that I couldn't reciprocate. . . . So I asked around where
I could get some and picked up for the first time.

Also, purchasing from a dealer is more economical, since there
are no middlemen and the purchaser of larger quantities
receives, as in the ordinary business world, a lower price.

However, in order to make these purchases, the user must
have a "connection"—know someone who makes a business
of selling drugs. Dealers operate illicitly, and in order to do
business with them one must know where to find them and be
identified to them in such a way that they will not hesitate to
make a sale. This is quite difficult for persons who are casually
involved in drug-using groups. But as a person becomes more
identified with these groups, and is considered more trust-
worthy, the necessary knowledge and introductions to dealers
become available to him. In becoming defined as a member,
one is also defined as a person who can safely be trusted to
buy drugs without endangering anyone else.

Even when the opportunity is made available to them,
many do not make use of it. The danger of arrest latent in such
an act prevents them from attempting it:

If it were freely distributed, I think that I would probably
keep it on hand all the time. But . . . [You mean if it wasn't
against the law?] Yeah. [Well, so does that mean that you don't

want to get involved . . .] Well, I don't want to get too involved, you know. I don't want to get too close to the people who traffic in, rather heavily in it. I've never had any difficulty much in getting any stuff. I just . . . someone usually has some and you can get it when you want it. Why, just why, I've never happened to run into those more or less direct contacts, the pushers, I suppose you'd explain it on the basis of the fact that I never felt the need for scrounging or looking up one.

Such fears operate only so long as the attempt is not made, for once it has been successfully accomplished the individual is able to use the experience to revise his estimate of the danger involved; the notion of danger no longer prevents purchase. Instead, the act is approached with a realistic caution which recognizes without overemphasizing the possibility of arrest. The purchaser feels safe so long as he observes elementary, common-sense precautions. Although many of the interviewees had made purchases, only a few reported any difficulty of a legal kind and these attributed it to the failure to take precautions.

For those who do establish connections, regular use is often interrupted by the arrest or disappearance of the man from whom they purchase their supply. In such circumstances, regular use can continue only if the user is able to find a new source of supply. This young man had to give up use for a while when:

Well, like Tom went to jail, they put him in jail. Then Cramer, how did it happen . . . Oh yeah, like I owed him some money and I didn't see him for quite a while and when I did try to see him he had moved and I couldn't find out from anyone where the cat went. So that was that connection . . ." [So you just didn't know where to get it?] No. [So you stopped?] Yeah.

The instability of sources of supply is an important control over regular use, and reflects indirectly the use of legal sanctions by the community in the arrest of those trafficking in drugs. Enforcement of the law controls use not by directly deterring users, but by rendering sources of the drug undependable and thus making access more difficult.

Each level of use, from beginning to routine, thus has its typical mode of supply, which must be present for such use to occur. In this sense, the social mechanisms which operate to limit availability of the drug limit its use. However, participation in groups in which marihuana is used creates the conditions under which the controls which limit access to it no longer operate. Such participation also involves increased sensitivity to the controls of the drug-using group, so that there are forces pressing toward use of the new sources of supply. Changes in the mode of supply in turn create the conditions for movement to a new level of use. Consequently, it may be said that changes in group participation and membership lead to changes in level of use by affecting the individual's access to marihuana under present conditions in which the drug is available only through illicit outlets.

Secrecy

Marihuana use is limited also to the extent that individuals actually find it inexpedient or believe that they will find it so. This inexpediency, real or presumed, arises from the fact or belief that if nonusers discover that one uses the drug, sanctions of some important kind will be applied. The user's conception of these sanctions is vague, because few users seem ever to have had such an experience or to have known anyone who did; most marihuana users are secret deviants. Although the user does not know what specifically to expect in the way of punishments, the outlines are clear: he fears repudiation by people whose respect and acceptance he requires both practically and emotionally. That is, he expects that his relationships with nonusers will be disturbed and disrupted if they should find out, and limits and controls his behavior to the degree that relationships with outsiders are important to him.

This kind of control breaks down in the course of the user's participation with other users and in the development of his experience with the drug, as he comes to realize that, though it might be true that sanctions would be applied if nonusers found out, they need never find out. At each level of use, there is a growth in this realization which makes the new level possible.

For the beginner, these considerations are very important and must be overcome if use is to be undertaken at all. His fears are challenged by the sight of others—more experienced users—who apparently feel there is little or no danger and appear to engage in the activity with impunity. If one does "try it once," he may still his fears by observations of this kind. Participation with other users thus furnishes the beginner with the rationalizations with which first to attempt the act.

Further participation in marihuana use allows the novice to draw the further conclusion that the act can be safe no matter how often indulged in, as long as one is careful and makes sure that nonusers are not present or likely to intrude. This kind of perspective is a necessary prerequisite for occasional use, in which the drug is used when other users invite one to join them. While it permits this level of use, such a perspective does not allow regular use to occur for the worlds of user and nonuser, while separate to a degree allowing the occasional use pattern to persist, are not completely segregated. The points where these worlds meet appear dangerous to the occasional user who must, therefore, confine his use to those occasions on which such meeting does not seem likely.

Regular use, on the other hand, implies a systematic and routine use of the drug which does not take into account such possibilities and plan periods of getting high around them. It is a mode of use which depends on another kind of attitude toward the possibility of nonusers finding out, the attitude that marihuana use can be carried on under the noses of nonusers or, alternatively, on the living of a pattern of social participation which reduces contacts with nonusers almost to the zero point. Without this adjustment in attitude, paricipation, or both, the user is forced to remain at the level of occasional use. These adjustments take place in terms of two categories of risks involved: first, that nonusers will discover marihuana in one's possession and, second, that one will be unable to hide the effects of the drug when he is high while with nonusers.

The difficulties of the would-be regular user, in terms of possession, are illustrated in the remarks of a young man who unsuccessfully attempted regular use while living with his parents:

I never did like to have it around the house, you know. [Why?] Well, I thought maybe my mother might find it or something like that. [What do you think she'd say?] Oh, well, you know, like . . . well, they never do mention it, you know, anything about dope addicts or anything like that but it would be a really bad thing in my case, I know, because of the big family I come from. And my sisters and brothers, they'd put me down the worst. [And you don't want that to happen?] No, I'm afraid not.

In such cases, envisioning the consequences of such a secret being discovered prevents the person from maintaining the supply essential to regular use. Use remains erratic, since it must depend on encounters with other users and cannot occur whenever the user desires.

Unless he discovers some method of overcoming this difficulty, the person can progress to regular use only when the relationship deterring use is broken. People do not ordinarily leave their homes and families in order to smoke marihuana regularly. But if they do, for whatever reason, regular use, heretofore proscribed, becomes a possibility. Confirmed regular users often take into very serious account the effect on their drug use of forming new social relationships with nonusers:

I wouldn't marry someone who would be belligerent if I do [smoke marihuana], you know. I mean, I wouldn't marry a woman who would be so untrusting as to think I would do something . . . I mean, you know, like hurt myself or try to hurt someone.

If such attachments are formed, use tends to revert to the occasional level:

[This man had used marihuana quite intensively but his wife objected to it.] Of course, largely the reason I cut off was my wife. There were a few times when I'd feel like . . . didn't actually crave for it but would just like to have had some. [He was unable to continue using the drug except irregularly, on those occasions when he was away from his wife's presence and control.]

If the person moves almost totally into the user group, the problem ceases in many respects to exist, and it is possible for regular use to occur except when some new connection with the more conventional world is made.

If a person uses marihuana regularly and routinely it is almost inevitable—since even in urban society such roles cannot be kept completely separate—that he one day find himself high while in the company of nonusers from whom he wishes to keep his marihuana use secret. Given the variety of symptoms the drug may produce, it is natural for the user to fear that he might reveal through his behavior that he is high, that he might be unable to control the symptoms and thus give away his secret. Such phenomena as difficulty in focusing one's attention and in carrying on normal conversation create a fear that everyone will know exactly why one is behaving this way, that the behavior will be interpreted automatically as a sign of drug use.

Those who progress to regular use manage to avoid this dilemma. It may happen, as noted above, that they come to participate almost completely in the subcultural group in which the practice is carried on, so that they simply have a minimal amount of contact with nonusers about whose opinions they care. Since this isolation from conventional society is seldom complete, the user must learn another method of avoiding the dilemma, one which is the most important method for those whose participation is never so completely segregated. This consists in learning to control the drug's effects while in the company of nonusers, so that they can be fooled and the secret successfully kept even though one continues participation with them. If one cannot learn this, there exists some group of situations in which he dare not get high and regular use is not possible:

Say, I'll tell you something that just kills me, man, I mean it's really terrible. Have you ever got high and than had to face your family? I really dread that. Like having to talk to my father or mother, or brothers, man, it's just too much. I just can't make it. I just feel like they're sitting there digging [watching] me, and they know I'm high. It's a horrible feeling. I hate it.

Most users have these feelings and move on to regular use, if they do, only if an experience of the following order occurs, changing their conception of the possibilities of detection:

[Were you making it much then, at first?] No, not too much. Like I said, I was a little afraid of it. But it was finally about 1948 that I really began to make it strong. [What were you afraid of?]

Well, I was afraid that I would get high and not be able to op [operate], you dig, I mean, I was afraid to let go and see what would happen. Especially on jobs. I couldn't trust myself when I was high. I was afraid I'd get too high, and pass out completely, or do stupid things. I didn't want to get too wigged.

[How did you ever get over that?] Well, it's just one of those things, man. One night I turned on and I just suddenly felt real great, relaxed, you know, I was really swinging with it. From then on I've just been able to smoke as much as I want without getting into any trouble with it. I can always control it.

The typical experience is one in which the user finds himself in a position where he must do something while he is high that he is quite sure he cannot do in that condition. To his surprise, he finds he can do it and can hide from others the fact that he is under the drug's influence. One or more occurrences of this kind allow the user to conclude that he can remain a secret deviant, that his caution has been excessive and based on a false premise. If he desires to use the drug regularly he is no longer deterred by this fear, for he can use such an experience to justify the belief that nonusers need never know:

[I suggested that many users find it difficult to perform their work tasks effectively while high. The interviewee, a machinist, replied with the story of how he got over this barrier.]

It doesn't bother me that way. I had an experience once that proved that to me. I was out on a pretty rough party the night before. I got pretty high. On pot [marihuana] and lushing, too. I got so high that I was still out of my mind when I went to work the next day. And I had a very important job to work on. It had to be practically perfect—precision stuff. The boss had been priming me for it for days, explaining how to do it and everything.

[He went to work high and, as far as he could remember, must have done the job, although there was no clear memory of it since he was still quite high.]

About a quarter to four, I finally came down and I thought, "Jesus! What am I doing?" So I just cut out and went, home. I didn't sleep all night hardly, worrying about whether I had

71

fucked up on that job or not. I got down the next morning, the boss puts the old "mikes" on the thing, and I had done the fuckin' job perfectly. So after that I just didn't worry any more. I've gone down to work really out of my mind on some mornings. I don't have any trouble at all.

The problem is not equally important for all users, for there are those whose social participation is such that it cannot arise; they are completely integrated into the deviant group. All their associates know they use marihuana and none of them care, while their conventional contacts are few and unimportant. In addition, some persons achieve idiosyncratic solutions which allow them to act high and have it ignored:

They [the boys in his neighborhood] can never tell if I'm high. I usually am, but they don't know it. See, I always had the reputation, all through high school, of being kind of goofy, so no matter what I do, nobody pays much attention. So I can get away with being high practically anyplace.

In short, persons limit their use of marihuana in proportion to the degree of their fear, realistic or otherwise, that nonusers who are important to them will discover they use drugs and react in some punishing way. This kind of control breaks down as the user discovers his fears are excessive and unrealistic, as he comes to conceive the practice as one which can be kept secret with relative ease. Each level of use can occur only when the person has revised his conception of the dangers involved in such a way as to allow it.

Morality

Conventional notions of morality are another means through which marihuana use is controlled. The basic moral imperatives which operate here are those which require the individual to be responsible for his own welfare, and to be able to control his behavior rationally. The stereotype of the dope fiend portrays a person who violates these imperatives. A recent description of the marihuana user illustrates the principal features of this stereotype:

In the earliest stages of intoxication the will power is destroyed and inhibitions and restraints are released; the moral barricades are broken down and often debauchery and sexuality result. Where mental instability is inherent, the behavior is generally violent. An egotist will enjoy delusions of grandeur, the timid individual will suffer anxiety, and the aggressive one often will resort to acts of violence and crime. Dormant tendencies are released and while the subject may know what is happening, he has become powerless to prevent it. Constant use produces an incapacity for work and a disorientation of purpose.[1]

One must add to this, of course, the notion that the user becomes a slave to the drug, that he voluntarily surrenders himself to a habit from which there is no escape. The person who takes such a stereotype seriously is presented with an obstacle to drug use. He will not begin, maintain, or increase his use of marihuana unless he can neutralize his sensitivity to the stereotype by accepting an alternative view of the practice. Otherwise he will, as would most members of the society, condemn himself as a deviant outsider.

The beginner has at some time shared the conventional view. In the course of his participation in an unconventional segment of society, however, he is likely to acquire a more "emancipated" view of the moral standards implicit in the usual characterization of the drug user, at least to the point that he will not reject activities out of hand simply because they are conventionally condemned. The observation of others

1. H. J. Anslinger and William F. Tompkins, *The Traffic in Narcotics* (New York: Funk and Wagnalls Co., 1953), pp. 21–22.

using the drug may further tempt him to apply his rejection of conventional standards to the specific instance of marihuana use. Such participation, then, tends to provide the conditions under which controls can be circumvented at least sufficiently for first use to be attempted.

In the course of further experience in drug-using groups, the novice acquires a series of rationalizations and justifications with which he may answer objections to occasional use if he decides to engage in it. If he should himself raise the objections of conventional morality he finds ready answers available in the folklore of marihuana-using groups.

One of the most common rationalizations is that conventional persons indulge in much more harmful practices and that a comparatively minor vice like marihuana smoking cannot really be wrong when such things as the use of alcohol are so commonly accepted:

[You don't dig alcohol then?] No, I don't dig it at all. [Why not?] I don't know. I just don't. Well, see, here's the thing. Before I was at the age where kids start drinking I was already getting on [using marihuana] and I saw the advantages of getting on, you know, I mean there was no sickness and it was much cheaper. That was one of the first things I learned, man. Why do you want to drink? Drinking is dumb, you know. It's so much cheaper to get on and you don't get sick, and it's not sloppy and takes less time. And it just grew to be the thing, you know. So I got on before I drank, you know. . . .

[What do you mean that's one of the first things you learned?] Well, I mean, as I say, I was just first starting to play jobs as a musician when I got on and I was also in a position to drink on the jobs, you know. And these guys just told me it was silly to drink. They didn't drink either.

Additional rationalizations enable the user to suggest to himself that the drug's effects, rather than being harmful, are in fact beneficial:

I have had some that made me feel like . . . very invigorated and also it gives a very strong appetite. It makes you very hungry. That's probably good for some people who are underweight.

Finally, the user, at this point, is not using the drug all the time. His use is scheduled; there are times when he considers it appropriate and times when he does not. The existence of this schedule allows him to assure himself that he controls the drug and becomes a symbol of the harmlessness of the practice. He does not consider himself a slave to the drug, because he can and does abide by his schedule, no matter how much use the particular schedule may allow. The fact that there are times when he does not, on principle, use the drug, can be used as proof to himself of his freedom with respect to it.

I like to get on and mostly do get on when I'm relaxing, doing something I enjoy like listening to a real good classical record or maybe like a movie or something like that or listening to a radio program. Something I enjoy doing, not participating in, like . . . I play golf during the summer, you know, and a couple of guys I play with got on, turned on while they were playing golf and I couldn't see that because, I don't know, when you're participating in something you want your mind to be on that and nothing else, and if you're . . . because I think, I know it makes you relax and . . . I don't think you can make it as well.

Occasional use can occur in an individual who accepts these views, for he has reorganized his moral notions in such a way as to permit it, primarily by acquiring the conception that conventional moral notions about drugs do not apply to this drug and that, in any case, his use of it has not become excessive.

If use progresses to the point of becoming regular and systematic, moral questions may again be raised for the user, for he begins now to look, to himself as well as others, like the uncontrolled "dope fiend" of popular mythology. He must convince himself again, if regular use is to continue, that he has not crossed this line. The problem, and one possible resolution, are presented in a statement by a regular user:

I know it isn't habit forming but I was a little worried about how easy it would be to put down, so I tried it. I was smoking it all the time, then I just put it down for a whole week to see what would happen. Nothing happened. So I knew it was cool [all right]. Ever since then I've used it as much as I want to. Of course, I wouldn't dig being a slave to it or anything like that, but I don't think that that would happen unless I was neurotic or something, and I don't think I am, not to that extent.

The earlier rationalization that the drug has beneficial effects remains unchanged and may even undergo a considerable elaboration. But the question raised in the last quotation proves more troublesome. In view of his increased and regularized consumption of the drug, the user is not sure that he is really able to control it, that he has not perhaps become the slave of a vicious habit. Tests are made—use is given up and the consequences awaited—and when nothing untoward occurs, the user is able to draw the conclusion that there is nothing to fear.

The problem is, however, more difficult for some of the more sophisticated users who derive their moral directives not so much from conventional thinking as from popular psychiatric "theory." Their use troubles them, not in conventional terms, but because of what it may indicate about their mental health. Accepting current thinking about the causes of drug use, they reason that no one would use drugs in large amounts unless "something" were "wrong" with him, unless there were some neurotic maladjustment which made drugs necessary. The fact of marihuana smoking becomes a symbol of psychic weakness and, ultimately, moral weakness. This prejudices the person against further regular use and causes a return to occasional use unless a new rationale is discovered.

Well, I wonder if the best thing is not to get on anything at all. That's what they tell you. Although I've heard psychiatrists say, "Smoke all the pot you want, but leave the horse [heroin] alone."

[Well, that sounds reasonable.] Yeah, but how many people can do it? There aren't very many . . . I think that seventy-five per cent or maybe even a bigger per cent of the people that turn on have a behavior pattern that would lead them to get on more and more pot to get more and more away from things. I think I have it myself. But I think I'm aware of it so I think I can fight it.

The notion that to be aware of the problem is to solve it constitutes a self-justifying rationale in the above instance. Where justifications cannot be discovered, use continues on an occasional basis, the user explaining his reasons in terms of his conception of psychiatric theory:

Well, I believe that people who indulge in narcotics and alcohol and drinks, any stimulants of that type, on that level, are probably looking for an escape from a more serious condition than the more or less occasional user. I don't feel that I'm escaping from anything. I think that, however, I realize that I have a lot of adjustment to accomplish yet. . . . So I can't say that I have any serious neurotic condition or inefficiency that I'm trying to handle. But in the case of some acquaintances I've made, people who are chronic alcoholics or junkies [opiate addicts] or pretty habitual smokers, I have found accompanying that condition some maladjustment in their personality, too.

Certain morally toned conceptions about the nature of drug use and drug users thus influence the marihuana user. If he is unable to explain away or ignore these conceptions, use will not occur at all; and the degree of use appears to be related to the degree to which the conceptions are no longer influential, having been replaced by rationalizations and justifications current among users.

In short, a person will feel free to use marihuana to the degree that he comes to regard conventional conceptions of it as the uninformed views of outsiders and replaces those conceptions with the "inside" view he has acquired through his experience with the drug in the company of other users.

5 The Culture of a Deviant Group

THE DANCE MUSICIAN

ALTHOUGH deviant behavior is often proscribed by law—labeled criminal if engaged in by adults or delinquent if engaged in by youths—this need not be the case. Dance musicians, whose culture we investigate in this and the next chapter, are a case in point. Though their activities are formally within the law, their culture and way of life are sufficiently bizarre and unconventional for them to be labeled as outsiders by more conventional members of the community.

Many deviant groups, among them dance musicians, are stable and long-lasting. Like all stable groups, they develop a distinctive way of life. To understand the behavior of someone who is a member of such a group it is necessary to understand that way of life.

Robert Redfield expressed the anthropologist's view of culture this way:

> In speaking of "culture" we have reference to the conventional understandings, manifest in act and artifact, that characterize societies. The "understandings" are the meanings attached to acts and objects. The meanings are conventional, and therefore cultural in so far as they have become typical for the members of that society by reason of inter-communication among the members. A culture is, then, an abstraction: it is the type toward which the meanings that the same act or object has for the different members of the society tend to conform. The meanings are expressed in action and in the results of action, from which we infer them; so we may as well identify "culture" with the extent to which the conventionalized behavior of members of the society is for all the same.[1]

Hughes has noted that the anthropological view of culture seems best suited to the homogeneous society, the primitive society on which the anthropologist works. But the term, in the sense of an organization of common understandings held by a group, is equally applicable to the smaller groups that make up a complex modern society. Ethnic groups, religious groups, regional groups, occupational groups—each of these can be shown to have certain kinds of common understandings and thus a culture.

Wherever some group of people have a bit of common life with a modicum of isolation from other people, a common corner in society, common problems and perhaps a couple of common enemies, there culture grows. It may be the fantastic culture of the unfortunates who, having become addicted to the use of heroin, share a forbidden pleasure, a tragedy and a battle against the conventional world. It may be the culture of a pair of infants who, in coping with the same all powerful and arbitrary parents, build up a language and a set of customs of their own

1. Robert Redfield, *The Folk Culture of Yucatan* (Chicago: University of Chicago Press, 1941), p. 132.

which persist even when they are as big and powerful as the parents. It may be the culture of a group of students who, ambitious to become physicians, find themselves faced with the same cadavers, quizzes, puzzling patients, instructors and deans.[2]

Many people have suggested that culture arises essentially in response to a problem faced in common by a group of people, insofar as they are able to interact and communicate with one another effectively.[3] People who engage in activities regarded as deviant typically have the problem that their view of what they do is not shared by other members of the society. The homosexual feels his kind of sex life is proper, but others do not. The thief feels it is appropriate for him to steal, but no one else does. Where people who engage in deviant activities have the opportunity to interact with one another they are likely to develop a culture built around the problems rising out of the differences between their definition of what they do and the definition held by other members of the society. They develop perspectives on themselves and their deviant activities and on their relations with other members of the society. (Some deviant acts, of course, are committed in isolation and the people who commit them have no opportunity to develop a culture. Examples of this might be the compulsive pyromaniac or the kleptomaniac.[4]) Since these cultures operate within,

2. Everett Cherrington Hughes, *Students' Culture and Perspectives: Lectures on Medical and General Education* (Lawrence, Kansas: University of Kansas Law School, 1961), pp. 28–29.

3. See Albert K. Cohen, *Delinquent Boys: The Culture of the Gang* (New York: The Free Press of Glencoe, 1955); Richard A. Cloward and Lloyd E. Ohlin, *Delinquency and Opportunity: A Theory of Delinquent Gangs* (New York: The Free Press of Glencoe, 1960); and Howard S. Becker, Blanche Geer, Everett C. Hughes, and Anselm L. Strauss, *Boys in White: Student Culture in Medical School* (Chicago: University of Chicago Press, 1961).

4. Donald R. Cressey, "Role Theory, Differential Association, and Compulsive Crimes," in Arnold M. Rose, editor, *Human Behavior and Social Processes: An Interactionist Approach* (Boston: Houghton Mifflin Co., 1962), pp. 444–467.

and in distinction to, the culture of the larger society, they are often called subcultures.

The dance musician, to whose culture or subculture this chapter is devoted, may be defined simply as someone who plays popular music for money. He is a member of a service occupation and the culture he participates in gets its character from the problems common to service occupations. The service occupations are, in general, distinguished by the fact that the worker in them comes into more or less direct and personal contact with the ultimate consumer of the product of his work, the client for whom he performs the service. Consequently, the client is able to direct or attempt to direct the worker at his task and to apply sanctions of various kinds, ranging from informal pressure to the withdrawal of his patronage and the conferring of it on some others of the many people who perform the service.

Service occupations bring together a person whose full-time activity is centered around the occupation and whose self is to some degree deeply involved in it, and another person whose relation to it is much more casual. It may be inevitable that the two should have widely varying pictures of the way the occupational service should be performed. Members of service occupations characteristically consider the client unable to judge the proper worth of the service and bitterly resent attempts on his part to exercise control over the work. Conflict and hostility arise as a result, methods of defense against outside interference become a preoccupation of the members, and a subculture grows around this set of problems.

Musicians feel that the only music worth playing is what they call "jazz," a term which can be partially defined as that music which is produced without reference to the demands of outsiders. Yet they must endure unceasing interference with their playing by employers and audience. The most distressing problem in the career of the average musician, as we shall see later, is the necessity of choosing between conventional success and his artistic standards. In order to achieve success he finds it necessary to "go commercial," that is, to play in accord with the wishes of the nonmusicians for whom he works; in doing so he sacrifices the respect of other musicians and thus, in most cases, his self-respect. If he remains true to his standards, he is usually doomed to failure in the larger society. Musicians classify themselves according to the degree to which they give in to outsiders; the continuum ranges from the extreme "jazz" musician to the "commercial" musician.

Below I will focus on the following points: (1) the conceptions that musicians have of themselves and of the nonmusicians for whom they work and the conflict they feel to be inherent in this relation; (2) the basic consensus underlying the reactions of both commercial and jazz musicians to this conflict; and (3) the feelings of isolation musicians have from the larger society and the way they segregate themselves from audience and community. The problems arising out of the difference between the musician's definition of his work and those of the people he works for may be taken as a prototype of the problems deviants have in dealing with outsiders who take a different view of their deviant activities.[5]

The Research

I gathered the material for this study by participant observation, by participating with musicians in the variety of situa-

5. For other studies of the jazz musician, see: Carlo L. Lastrucci, "The Professional Dance Musician," *Journal of Musicology*, III (Winter, 1941), 168–172; William Bruce Cameron, "Sociological Notes on the Jam Session," *Social Forces*, XXXIII (December, 1954), 177–182; and Alan P. Merriam and Raymond W. Mack, "The Jazz Community," *Social Forces*, XXXVIII (March, 1960), 211–222.

tions that made up their work and leisure lives. At the time I made the study I had played the piano professionally for several years and was active in musical circles in Chicago. This was in 1948 and 1949, a period when many musicians were taking advantage of their benefits under the G.I. Bill, so the fact that I was going to college did not differentiate me from others in the music business. I worked with many different orchestras and many different kinds of orchestras during that period and kept extensive notes on the events that occurred while I was with other musicians. Most of the people I observed did not know that I was making a study of musicians. I seldom did any formal interviewing, but concentrated rather on listening to and recording the ordinary kinds of conversation that occurred among musicians. Most of my observation was carried out on the job, and even on the stand as we played. Conversations useful for my purposes often took place also at the customary "job markets" in the local union offices where musicians looking for work and band leaders looking for men to hire gathered on Monday and Saturday afternoons.

The world of the dance musician is a highly differentiated one. Some men work mostly in bars and taverns, either in outlying neighborhoods or in the downtown area. Some play with larger bands in ballrooms and night clubs. Others do not work steadily in one place, but work with orchestras that play for private dances and parties in hotels and country clubs. Still other men play with nationally known "name" bands or work in radio and television studios. Men who work in each kind of job setting have problems and attitudes that are in part characteristic of that setting. I worked mostly in bars, taverns, and occasionally with various kinds of "jobbing" bands. But I had enough contact with members of other groups, through meetings on occasional dance jobs and at the union hall, to be able to get evidence on their attitudes and activities as well.

Since completing the research, I have worked as a musician in two other locations, a small university town (Champaign-Urbana, Illinois) and a large city, though not so large as Chicago (Kansas City, Missouri). There are differences in the organization of the music business associated with the differences in size of these cities. In Chicago, it is much more possible for a musician to specialize. He may be a ballroom musician, or work only in taverns and night clubs (as I did). In the smaller towns, there is not as much work of any one kind and, furthermore, there are fewer musicians in proportion to the population. Therefore, one musician may be called on to perform in any of the several settings I have described, either because he has little choice of where to play or because the leader looking for someone to work for him has little choice among the available musicians. Although I have not kept formal notes on my experiences in these other settings. none of them furnished data that would require changes in the conclusions I reached on the basis of the Chicago materials.

Musician and "Square"

The system of beliefs about what musicians are and what audiences are is summed up in a word used by musicians to refer to outsiders—"square." It is used as a noun and as an adjective, denoting both a kind of person and a quality of behavior and objects. The term refers to the kind of person who is the opposite of all the musician is, or should be, and a way of thinking, feeling, and behaving (with its expression in material objects) which is the opposite of that valued by musicians.

The musician is conceived of as an artist who possesses a mysterious artistic gift setting him apart from all other people.

Possessing this gift, he should be free from control by outsiders who lack it. The gift is something which cannot be acquired through education; the outsider, therefore, can never become a member of the group. A trombone player said, "You can't teach a guy to have a beat. Either he's got one or he hasn't. If he hasn't got it, you can't teach it to him."

The musician feels that under no circumstances should any outsider be allowed to tell him what to play or how to play it. In fact, the strongest element in the colleague code is the prohibition against criticizing or in any other way trying to put pressure on another musician in the actual playing situation "on the job." Where not even a colleague is permitted to influence the work, it is unthinkable that an outsider should be allowed to do so.

This attitude is generalized into a feeling that musicians are different from and better than other kinds of people and accordingly ought not to be subject to the control of outsiders in any branch of life, particularly in their artistic activity. The feeling of being a different kind of person who leads a different kind of life is deep-seated, as the following remarks indicate:

I'm telling you, musicians are different than other people. They talk different, they act different, they look different. They're just not like other people, that's all. . . . You know it's hard to get out of the music business because you feel so different from others.

Musicians live an exotic life, like in a jungle or something. They start out, they're just ordinary kids from small towns—but once they get into that life they change. It's like a jungle, except that their jungle is a hot, crowded bus. You live that kind of life long enough, you just get to be completely different.

Being a musician was great, I'll never regret it. I'll understand things that squares never will.

An extreme of this view is the belief that only musicians are sensitive and unconventional enough to be able to give real sexual satisfaction to a woman.

Feeling their difference strongly, musicians likewise believe they are under no obligation to imitate the conventional behavior of squares. From the idea that no one can tell a musician how to play it follows logically that no one can tell a musician how to do anything. Accordingly, behavior which flouts conventional social norms is greatly admired. Stories reveal this admiration for highly individual, spontaneous, devil-may-care activities; many of the most noted jazzmen are renowned as "characters," and their exploits are widely recounted. For example, one well-known jazzman is noted for having jumped on a policeman's horse standing in front of the night club in which he worked and ridden it away. The ordinary musician likes to tell stories of unconventional things he has done:

We played the dance and after the job was over we packed up to get back in this old bus and make it back to Detroit. A little way out of town the car just refused to go. There was plenty of gas; it just wouldn't run. These guys all climbed out and stood around griping. All of a sudden, somebody said, "Let's set it on fire!" So someone got some gas out of the tanks and sprinkled it around, touching a match to it and whoosh, it just went up in smoke. What an experience! The car burning up and all these guys standing around hollering and clapping their hands. It was really something.

This is more than idiosyncrasy; it is a primary occupational value, as indicated by the following observation of a young musician: "You know, the biggest heroes in the music business are the biggest characters. The crazier a guy acts, the greater he is, the more everyone likes him."

As they do not wish to be forced to live in terms of social conventions, so musicians do not attempt to force these conventions on others. For example, a musician declared that ethnic discrimination is wrong, since every person is entitled to act and believe as he wants to:

Shit, I don't believe in any discrimination like that. People are people, whether they're Dagos or Jews or Irishmen or Polacks or what. Only big squares care what religion they are. It don't mean a fucking thing to me. Every person's entitled to believe his own way, that's the way I feel about it. Of course, I never go to church myself, but I don't hold it against anybody who does. It's all right if you like that sort of thing.

The same musician classified a friend's sex behavior as wrong, yet defended the individual's right to decide what is right and wrong for himself: "Eddie fucks around too much; he's gonna kill himself or else get killed by some broad. And he's got a nice wife too. He shouldn't treat her like that. But what the fuck, that's his business. If that's the way he wants to live, if he's happy that way, then that's the way he oughta do." Musicians will tolerate extraordinary behavior in a fellow-musician without making any attempt to punish or restrain him. In the following incident the uncontrolled behavior of a drummer loses a job for an orchestra; yet, angry as they are, they lend him money and refrain from punishing him in any way. It would be a breach of custom were anyone to reprimand him.

JERRY: When we got up there, the first thing that happened was that all his drums didn't show up. So the owner drives all around trying to find some drums for him and then the owner smashes a fender while he was doing it. So I knew right away that we were off to a good start. And Jack! Man, the boss is an old Dago, you know, no bullshit about him, he runs a gambling joint; he don't take any shit from anyone. So he says to Jack, "What are you gonna do without drums?" Jack says, "Be cool, daddio, everything'll be real gone, you know." I thought the old guy would blow his top. What a way to talk to the boss. Boy, he turned around, there was fire in his eye. I knew we wouldn't last after that. He says to me, "Is that drummer all there?" I said, "I don't know, I never saw him before today." And we just got finished telling him we'd been playing together six months.

So that helped, too. Of course, when Jack started playing, that was the end. So loud! And he don't play a beat at all. All he uses the bass drum for is accents. What kind of drumming is that? Otherwise, it was a good little outfit. . . . It was a good job. We could have been there forever. . . . Well, after we played a couple of sets, the boss told us we were through.

BECKER: What happened after you got fired?

JERRY: The boss gave us twenty apiece and told us to go home. So it cost us seventeen dollars for transportation up and back, we made three bucks on the job. Of course, we saw plenty of trees. Three bucks, hell, we didn't even make that. We loaned Jack seven or eight.

The musician thus views himself and his colleagues as people with a special gift which makes them different from nonmusicians and not subject to their control, either in musical performance or in ordinary social behavior.

The square, on the other hand, lacks this special gift and any understanding of the music or way of life of those who possess it. The square is thought of as an ignorant, intolerant person who is to be feared, since he produces the pressures forcing the musician to play inartistically. The musician's difficulty lies in the fact that the square is in a position to get his way: if he does not like the kind of music played, he does not pay to hear it a second time.

Not understanding music, the square judges music by standards foreign to musicians and not respected by them. A commercial saxophonist observed sarcastically:

It doesn't make any difference what we play, the way we do it. It's so simple that anyone who's been playing longer than a month could handle it. Jack plays a chorus on piano or something, then saxes or something, all unison. It's very easy. But the people don't care. As long as they can hear the drum they're all right. They hear the drum, then they know to put their right foot in front of their left foot and their left foot in front of their right foot. Then if they can hear the melody to whistle to, they're happy. What more could they want?

The following conversation illustrates the same attitude:

JOE: You'd get off the stand and walk down the aisle, somebody'd say, "Young man, I like your orchestra very much." Just because you played soft and the tenorman doubled fiddle or something like that, the squares liked it. . . .

DICK: It was like that when I worked at the M——— Club. All the kids that I went to high school with used to come out and dig the band. . . . That was one of the worst bands I ever worked on and they all thought it was wonderful.

JOE: Oh, well, they're just a bunch of squares anyhow.

"Squareness" is felt to penetrate every aspect of the square's behavior just as its opposite, "hipness," is evident in everything the musician does. The square seems to do everything wrong and is laughable and ludicrous. Musicians derive a good deal of amusement from sitting and watching squares. Everyone has stories to tell about the laughable antics of squares. One man went so far as to suggest that the musicians should change places with the people sitting at the bar of the tavern he worked in; he claimed they were funnier and more entertaining than he could possibly be. Every item of dress, speech, and behavior which differs from that of the musician is taken as new evidence of the inherent insensitivity and ignorance of the square. Since musicians have an esoteric culture these evidences are many and serve only to fortify their conviction that musicians and squares are two different kinds of people.

But the square is feared as well, since he is thought of as the ultimate source of commercial pressure. It is the square's ignorance of music that compels the musician to play what he considers bad music in order to be successful.

BECKER: How do you feel about the people you play for, the audience?

DAVE: They're a drag.

BECKER: Why do you say that?

DAVE: Well, if you're working on a commercial band, they like it and so you have to play more corn. If you're working on a good band, then they don't like it, and that's a drag. If you're working on a good band and they like it, then that's a drag, too. You hate them anyway, because you know that they don't know what it's all about. They're just a big drag.

This last statement reveals that even those who attempt to avoid being square are still considered so, because they still lack the proper understanding, which only a musician can have— "they don't know what it's all about." The jazz fan is thus respected no more than other squares. His liking for jazz is without understanding and he acts just like the other squares; He will request songs and try to influence the musician's playing, just as other squares do.

The musician thus sees himself as a creative artist who should be free from outside control, a person different from and better than those outsiders he calls squares who understand neither his music nor his way of life and yet because of whom he must perform in a manner contrary to his professional ideals.

Reactions to the Conflict

Jazz and commercial musicians agree in essentials on their attitude toward the audience, although they vary in the way they phrase this basic consensus. Two conflicting themes constitute the basis of agreement: (1) the desire for free self-expression in accord with the beliefs of the musician group, and (2) the recognition that outside pressures may force the musician to forego satisfying that desire. The jazzman tends to emphasize the first, the commercial musician the second; but both recognize and feel the force of each of these guiding influences. Common to the attitudes of both kinds of musician is an intense contempt for and dislike of the square audience whose fault it is that musicians must "go commercial" in order to succeed.

The commercial musician, though he conceives of the audience as square, chooses to sacrifice self-respect and the respect of other musicians (the rewards of artistic behavior) for the more substantial rewards of steady work, higher income, and the prestige enjoyed by the man who goes commercial. One commercial musician commented:

They've got a nice class of people out here, too. Of course, they're squares, I'm not trying to deny that. Sure, they're a bunch of fucking squares, but who the fuck pays the bills? They pay 'em, so you gotta play what they want. I mean, what the shit, you can't make a living if you don't play for the squares. How many fucking people you think aren't squares? Out of a hundred people you'd be lucky if 15 per cent weren't squares. I mean, maybe professional people—doctors, lawyers, like that— they might not be square, but the average person is just a big fucking square. Of course, show people aren't like that. But outside of show people and professional people, everybody's a fucking square.[6] They don't know anything.

I'll tell you. This is something I learned about three years ago. If you want to make any money you gotta please the squares. They're the ones that pay the bills, and you gotta play for them. A good musician can't get a fucking job. You gotta play a bunch of shit. But what the fuck, let's face it. I want to live good. I want to make some money; I want a car, you know. How long can you fight it? . . .

Don't get me wrong. If you can make money playing jazz, great. But how many guys can do it? . . . If you can play jazz, great, like I said. But if you're on a bad fucking job, there's no sense fighting it, you gotta be commercial. I mean, the squares are paying your salary, so you might as well get used to it, they're the ones you gotta please.

6. Most musicians would not admit these exceptions.

92

Note that the speaker admits it is more "respectable" to be independent of the squares, and expresses contempt for the audience, whose squareness is made responsible for the whole situation.

These men phrase the problem primarily in economic terms: "I mean, shit, if you're playing for a bunch of squares you're playing for a bunch of squares. What the fuck are you gonna do? You can't push it down their throats. Well, I suppose you can make 'em eat it, but after all, they *are* paying you."

The jazzman feels the need to satisfy the audience just as strongly, although maintaining that one should not give in to it. Jazzmen, like others, appreciate steady jobs and good jobs and know they must satisfy the audience to get them, as the following conversation between two young jazzmen illustrates:

CHARLIE: There aren't any jobs where you can blow jazz. You have to play rumbas and pops [popular songs] and everything. You can't get anywhere blowing jazz. Man. I don't want to scuffle all my life.

EDDIE: Well, you want to enjoy yourself, don't you? You won't be happy playing commercial. You know that.

CHARLIE: I guess there's just no way for a cat to be happy. 'Cause it sure is a drag blowing commercial, but it's an awful drag not ever doing anything and playing jazz.

EDDIE: Jesus, why can't you be successful playing jazz? . . . I mean, you could have a great little outfit and still play arrangements, but good ones, you know.

CHARLIE: You could never get a job for a band like that.

EDDIE: Well, you could have a sexy little bitch to stand up in front and sing and shake her ass at the bears [squares]. Then you could get a job. And you could still play great when she wasn't singing.

CHARLIE: Well, wasn't that what Q———'s band was like? Did you enjoy that? Did you like the way she sang?

EDDIE: No, man, but we played jazz, you know.

CHARLIE: Did you like the kind of jazz you were playing? It was kind of commercial, wasn't it?

EDDIE: Yeah, but it could have been great.

CHARLIE: Yeah, if it had been great, you wouldn't have kept on working. I guess we'll always just be unhappy. It's just the way things are. You'll always be drug with yourself. . . . There'll never be any kind of a really great job for a musician.

In addition to the pressure to please the audience which emanates from the musician's desire to maximize salary and income, there are more immediate pressures. It is often difficult to maintain an independent attitude. For example:

I worked an Italian wedding on the Southwest Side last night with Johnny Ponzi. We played about half an hour, doing the special arrangements they use, which are pretty uncommercial. Then an old Italian fellow (the father-in-law of the groom, as we later found out) began hollering, "Play some polkas, play some Italian music. Ah, you stink, you're lousy." Johnny always tries to avoid the inevitable on these wedding jobs, putting off playing the folk music as long as he can. I said, "Man, why don't we play some of that stuff now and get it over with?" Tom said, "I'm afraid if we start doing that we'll be doing it all night." Johnny said, "Look, Howard, the groom is a real great guy. He told us to play anything we want and not to pay any attention to what the people say, so don't worry about it. . . ."

The old fellow kept hollering and pretty soon the groom came up and said, "Listen, fellows. I know you don't want to play any of that shit and I don't want you to, but that's my father-in-law, see. The only thing is, I don't want to embarrass my wife for him, so play some Dago music to keep him quiet, will yuh?" Johnny looked around at us and made a gesture of resignation.

He said, "All right, let's play the *Beer Barrel Polka*." Tom said, "Oh shit! Here we go." We played it and then we played an Italian dance, the *Tarentelle*.

Sometimes the employer applies pressure which makes even an uncompromising jazzman give in, at least for the duration of the job:

I was playing solo for one night over at the Y——— on
———rd St. What a drag! The second set, I was playing *Sunny
Side*, I played the melody for one chorus, then I played a little
jazz. All of a sudden the boss leaned over the side of the bar and
hollered, "I'll kiss your ass if anybody in this place knows what
tune you're playing!" And everybody in the place heard him,
too. What a big square! What could I do? I didn't say anything,
just kept playing. Sure was a drag.

Somewhat inconsistently, the musician wants to feel that
he is reaching the audience and that they are getting some
enjoyment from his work, and this also leads him to give in
to audience demands. One man said:

I enjoy playing more when there's someone to play for. You
kind of feel like there isn't much purpose in playing if there's
nobody there to hear you. I mean, after all, that's what music's
for—for people to hear and get enjoyment from. That's why
I don't mind playing corny too much. If anyone enjoys it, then
I kind of get a kick out of it. I guess I'm kind of a ham. But I
like to make people happy that way.

This statement is somewhat extreme; but most musicians feel
it strongly enough to want to avoid the active dislike of the
audience: "That's why I like to work with Tommy. At least
when you get off the stand, everybody in the place doesn't
hate you. It's a drag to work under conditions like that, where
everybody in the place just hates the whole band."

Isolation and Self-Segregation

Musicians are hostile to their audiences, afraid that they
must sacrifice their artistic standards to the squares. They exhibit certain patterns of behavior and belief which may be
viewed as adjustments to this situation. These patterns of
isolation and self-segregation are expressed in the actual play-

ing situation and in participation in the social intercourse of the larger community. The primary function of this behavior is to protect the musician from the interference of the square audience and, by extension, of the conventional society. Its primary consequence is to intensify the musician's status as an outsider, through the operation of a cycle of increasing deviance. Difficulties with squares lead to increasing isolation which in turn increase the possibilities of further difficulties.

As a rule, the musician is spatially isolated from the audience. He works on a platform, which provides a physical barrier that prevents direct interaction. This isolation is welcomed because the audience, being made up of squares, is felt to be potentially dangerous. The musicians fear that direct contact with the audience can lead only to interference with the musical performance. Therefore, it is safer to be isolated and have nothing to do with them. Once, where such physical isolation was not provided, a player commented:

Another thing about weddings, man. You're right down on the floor, right in the middle of the people. You can't get away from them. It's different if you're playing a dance or in a bar. In a dancehall you're up on a stage where they can't get at you. The same thing in a cocktail lounge, you're up behind the bar. But a wedding—man, you're right in the middle of them.

Musicians, lacking the usually provided physical barriers, often improvise their own and effectively segregate themselves from their audience.

I had a Jewish wedding job for Sunday night. . . . When I arrived, the rest of the boys were already there. The wedding had taken place late, so that the people were just beginning to eat. We decided, after I had conferred with the groom, to play during dinner. We set up in a far corner of the hall. Jerry pulled the piano around so that it blocked off a small space, which was thus separated from the rest of the people. Tony set up his drums in this space, and Jerry and Johnny stood there while we played.

I wanted to move the piano so that the boys could stand out in front of it and be next to the audience, but Jerry said, half-jokingly, "No, man. I have to have some protection from the squares." So we left things as they were. . . .

Jerry had moved around in front of the piano but, again half-humorously, had put two chairs in front of him, which separated him from the audience. When a couple took the chairs to sit on, Jerry set two more in their place. Johnny said, "Man, why don't we sit on those chairs?" Jerry said, "No, man. Just leave them there. That's my barricade to protect me from the squares."

Many musicians almost reflexively avoid establishing contact with members of the audience. When walking among them, they habitually avoid meeting the eyes of squares for fear this will establish some relationship on the basis of which the square will then request songs or in some other way attempt to influence the musical performance. Some extend the behavior to their ordinary social activity, outside of professional situations. A certain amount of this is inevitable, since the conditions of work—late hours, great geographic mobility, and so on—make social participation outside of the professional group difficult. If one works while others sleep, it is difficult to have ordinary social intercourse with them. This was cited by a musician who had left the profession, in partial explanation of his action: "And it's great to work regular hours, too, where you can see people instead of having to go to work every night." Some younger musicians complain that the hours of work make it hard for them to establish contacts with "nice" girls, since they preclude the conventional date.

But much self-segregation develops out of the hostility toward squares. The attitude is seen in its extreme among the "X——Avenue Boys," a clique of extreme jazzmen who reject the American culture *in toto.* The quality of their feeling toward the outside world is indicated by one man's private title for his theme song: "If You Don't Like My Queer Ways You

Can Kiss My Fucking Ass." The ethnic makeup of the group indicated further that their adoption of extreme artistic and social attitudes was part of a total rejection of conventional American society. With few exceptions the men came from older, more fully assimilated national groups: Irish, Scandinavian, German, and English. Further, many of them were reputed to come from wealthy families and the higher social classes. In short, their rejection of commercialism in music and squares in social life was part of the casting aside of the total American culture by men who enjoyed a privileged position, but were unable to achieve a satisfactory personal adjustment within it.

Every interest of this group emphasized their isolation from the standards and interests of conventional society. They associated almost exclusively with other musicians and girls who sang or danced in night clubs in the North Clark Street area of Chicago and had little or no contact with the conventional world. They were described politically thus: "They hate this form of government anyway and think it's real bad." They were unremittingly critical of both business and labor, disillusioned with the economic structure, and cynical about the political process and contemporary political parties. Religion and marriage were rejected completely, as were American popular and serious culture, and their reading was confined solely to the more esoteric *avant garde* writers and philosophers. In art and symphonic music they were interested in only the most esoteric developments. In every case they were quick to point out that their interests were not those of the conventional society and that they were thereby differentiated from it. It is reasonable to assume that the primary function of these interests was to make this differentiation unmistakably clear.

Although isolation and self-segregation found their most

extreme development among the "X—— Avenue Boys," they were manifested by less deviant musicians as well. The feeling of being isolated from the rest of the society was often quite strong; the following conversation, which took place between two young jazzmen, illustrates two reactions to the sense of isolation.

EDDIE: You know, man, I hate people. I can't stand to be around squares. They drag me so much I just can't stand them.

CHARLIE: You shouldn't be like that, man. Don't let them drag you. Just laugh at them. That's what I do. Just laugh at everything they do. That's the only way you'll be able to stand it.

A young Jewish musician, who definitely identified himself with the Jewish community, nevertheless felt this professional isolation strongly enough to make the following statements.

You know, a little knowledge is a dangerous thing. That's what happened to me when I first started playing. I just felt like I knew too much. I sort of saw, or felt, that all my friends from the neighborhood were real square and stupid. . . .

You know, it's funny. When you sit on that stand up there, you feel so different from others. Like I can even understand how Gentiles feel toward Jews. You see these people come up and they look Jewish, or they have a little bit of an accent or something, and they ask for a rumba or some damn thing like that, and I just feel, "What damn squares, these Jews," just like I was a *goy* myself. That's what I mean when I say you learn too much being a musician. I mean, you see so many things and get such a broad outlook on life that the average person just doesn't have.

On another occasion the same man remarked:

You know, since I've been out of work I've actually gotten so that I can talk to some of these guys in the neighborhood.

[You mean you had trouble talking to them before?]

Well, I'd just stand around and not know what to say. It still sobers me up to talk to those guys. Everything they say seems real silly and uninteresting.

The process of self-segregation is evident in certain symbolic expressions, particularly in the use of an occupational slang which readily identifies the man who can use it properly as someone who is not square and as quickly reveals as an outsider the person who uses it incorrectly or not at all. Some words have grown up to refer to unique professional problems and attitudes of musicians, typical of them being the term "square." Such words enable musicians to discuss problems and activities for which ordinary language provides no adequate terminology. There are, however, many words which are merely substitutes for the more common expressions without adding any new meaning. For example, the following are synonyms for money: "loot," "gold," "geetz," and "bread." Jobs are referred to as "gigs." There are innumerable synonyms for marijuana, the most common being "gage," "pot," "charge," "tea," and "shit."

The function of such behavior is pointed out by a young musician who was quitting the business:

I'm glad I'm getting out of the business, though. I'm getting sick of being around musicians. There's so much ritual and ceremony junk. They have to talk a special language, dress different, and wear a different kind of glasses. And it just doesn't mean a damn thing except "we're different."

6 Careers in a Deviant Occupational Group

THE DANCE MUSICIAN

I HAVE already discussed, particularly in considering the development of marihuana use, the *deviant career* (the development, that is, of a pattern of deviant behavior). I would like now to consider the kinds of careers that develop among dance musicians, a group of "outsiders" that considers itself and is considered by others to be "different." But instead of concentrating on the genesis of deviant modes of behavior, I will ask what consequences for a person's occupational career stem from the fact that the occupational group within which he makes that career is a deviant one.

In using the concept of career to study the fate of the individual within occupational organizations, Hughes has defined it as "objectively . . . a series of statuses and clearly defined offices . . . typical sequences of position, achievement, responsibility, and even of adventure. . . . Subjectively, a career is the moving perspective in which the person sees his life as a whole and interprets the meaning of his various attributes, actions, and the things which happen to him." [1] Hall's discussion of the stages of the medical career focuses more specifically on the career as a series of adjustments to the "network of institutions, formal organizations, and informal relationships" in which the profession is practiced.[2]

The career lines characteristic of an occupation take their shape from the problems peculiar to that occupation. These, in turn, are a function of the occupation's position vis-à-vis other groups in the society. The major problems of musicians, as we have seen, revolve around maintaining freedom from control over artistic behavior. Control is exerted by the outsiders for whom musicians work, who ordinarily judge and react to the musician's performance on the basis of standards quite different from his. The antagonistic relationship between musicians and outsiders shapes the culture of the musician and likewise produces the major contingencies and crisis points in his career.

Studies of more conventional occupations such as medicine have shown that occupational success (as members of the occupation define it) depends on finding a position for oneself in that influential group or groups that controls rewards within the occupation, and that the actions and gestures of colleagues play a great part in deciding the outcome of any individual's career.[3] Musicians are no exception to this proposition, and I

1. Everett C. Hughes, "Institutional Office and the Person," *American Journal of Sociology*, XLIII (November, 1937), 409–410.
2. Oswald Hall, "The Stages of a Medical Career," *American Journal of Sociology*, LIII (March, 1948), 327.
3. See Everett C. Hughes, *French Canada in Transition* (Chicago: University of Chicago Press, 1943), pp. 52–53; and Melville Dalton, "Informal Factors in Career Achievement," *American Journal of Sociology*, LVI

shall begin by considering their definitions of occupational success and the way the development of musical careers depends on successful integration into the organization of the music business.

There is more to the story of the musician's career, however. The problem of freedom from outside control creates certain additional career contingencies and adds certain complications to the structure of the occupation; I consider these next.

Finally, the musician's family (both the one he is born into and the one he creates by marrying) has a major effect on his career.[4] Parents and wives are typically not musicians and, as outsiders, often fail to understand the nature of the musician's attachment to his work. The misunderstandings and disagreements that arise often change the direction of a man's career and, in some cases, bring it to an end.

Cliques and Success

The musician conceives of success as movement through a hierarchy of available jobs. Unlike the industrial or white-collar worker, he does not identify his career with one employer; he expects to change jobs frequently. An informally recognized ranking of these jobs—taking account of the income involved, the hours of work, and the degree of com-

---

(March, 1951), 407–415, for discussions of the influence of the colleague group on careers in industrial organizations; and Hall, *op. cit.*, for a similar analysis of colleague influence in the medical profession. Hall's concept of the "inner fraternity" refers to that group which is so able to exert greatest influence.

4. See the discussion in Howard S. Becker, "The Implications of Research on Occupational Careers for a Model of Household Decision-Making," in Nelson N. Foote, editor, *Household Decision Making* (New York: New York University Press, 1961), pp. 239–254; and Howard S. Becker and Anselm L. Strauss, "Careers, Personality, and Adult Socialization," *American Journal of Sociology*, LXII (November, 1956), 253–263.

munity recognition of achievement felt—constitutes the scale by which a musician measures his success according to the kind of job he usually holds.

At the bottom of this scale is the man who plays irregularly for small dances, wedding receptions, and similar affairs, and is lucky to make union wages. At the next level are those men who have steady jobs in "joints"—lower class taverns and night clubs, small "strip joints," etc.—where pay is low and community recognition lower. The next level is comprised of those men who have steady jobs with local bands in neighborhood ballrooms and small, "respectable" night clubs and cocktail lounges in better areas of the city. These jobs pay more than joint jobs and the man working them can expect to be recognized as successful in his community. Approximately equivalent to these are men who work in so-called "class B name" orchestras, the second rank of nationally known dance orchestras. The next level consists of men who work in "class A name" bands, and in local orchestras that play the best night clubs and hotels, large conventions, etc. Salaries are good, hours are easy, and the men can expect to be recognized as successful within and outside of the profession. The top positions in this scale are occupied by men who hold staff positions in radio and television stations and legitimate theaters. Salaries are high, hours short, and these jobs are recognized as the epitome of achievement in the local music world, and as jobs of high-ranking respectability by outsiders.

A network of informal, interlocking cliques allocates the jobs available at a given time. In securing work at any one level, or in moving up to jobs at a new level, one's position in the network is of great importance. Cliques are bound together by ties of mutual obligation, the members sponsoring each other for jobs, either hiring one another when they have the power or recommending one another to those who do the hiring for an orchestra. The recommendation is of great importance, since it is by this means that available individuals become known to those who hire; the person who is unknown will not be hired, and membership in cliques insures that one has many friends who will recommend one to the right people.

Clique membership thus provides the individual with steady employment. One man explained:

See, it works like this. My right hand here, that's five musicians. My left hand, that's five more. Now one of these guys over here gets a job. He picks the men for it from just these guys in this group. Whenever one of them gets a job, naturally he hires this guy. So you see how it works. They never hire anybody that isn't in the clique. If one of them works, they all work.

The musician builds and cements these relationships by getting jobs for other men and so obligating them to return the favor:

There were a couple of guys on this band that I've got good jobs for, and they've had them ever since. Like one of those trombone players. I got him on a good band. One of the trumpet players, too. . . . You know the way that works. A leader asks you for a man. If he likes the guy you give him, why every time he needs a man he'll ask you. That way you can get all your friends on.

Security comes from the number and quality of relationships so established. To have a career one must work; to enjoy the security of steady work one must have many "connections":

You have to make connections like that all over town, until it gets so that when anybody wants a man they call you. Then you're never out of work.

A certain similarity to the informal organization of medical practice should be noted. Musicians cooperate by recommending each other for jobs in much the same way that members of the medical "inner fraternity" cooperate by furnishing each other with patients.[5] The two institutional complexes differ, however, in that medical practice (in all except the largest cities) tends to revolve around a few large hospitals which one, or a few, such fraternities can control. In music, the number of possible foci is much greater, with a correspondingly greater proliferation of organization and, consequently, there are more opportunities for the individual to establish the right connections for himself and a lessening of the power of any particular clique.

In addition to providing a measure of job security for their members, cliques also provide routes by which one can move up through the levels of jobs. In several cliques observed, membership was drawn from more than one level of the hierarchy; thus men of lower position were able to associate with men from a higher level. When a job becomes available higher in the scale, a man of the lower level may be sponsored by a higher-ranking man who recommends him, or hires him, and takes the responsibility for the quality of his performance. A radio staff musician described the proccess in these terms:

Now the other way to be a success is to have a lot of friends. You have to play good, but you have to have friends on different bands and when someone leaves a band, why they're plugging to get you on. It takes a long time to work yourself up that way. Like I've been 10 years getting the job I have now.

If the man so sponsored performs successfully he can build up more informal relationships at the new level and thus get more jobs at that level. Successful performance on the job is necessary if he is to establish himself fully at the new level, and sponsors exhibit a great deal of anxiety over the perform-

5. Hall, *op. cit.*, p. 332.

ance of their protégés. The multiple sponsorship described in this incident from my field notes illustrates this anxiety and its sources in the obligations of colleagues:

A friend of mine asked me if I was working that night. When I told him no, he led me over to another guy who, in turn, led me to an old fellow with a strong Italian accent. This man said, "You play piano, huh?" I said, "Yes." He said, "You play good, huh?" I said, "Yes." He said, "You play good? Read pretty good?" I said, "Not bad. What kind of a deal is this?" He said, "It's at a club here in the Loop. It's nine to four-thirty, pays two-fifty an hour. You're sure you can handle it?" I said, "Sure!" He touched my shoulder and said, "OK. I just have to ask you all these questions. I mean, I don't know you, I don't know how you play, I just have to ask, you see?" I said, "Sure." He said, "You know, I have to make sure, it's a spot downtown. Well, here. You call this number and tell them Mantuno told you to call—Mantuno. See, I have to make sure you're gonna do good or else I'm gonna catch hell. Go on, call 'em now. Remember, Mantuno told you to call."

He gave me the number. I called and got the job. When I came out of the booth my friend who had originated the deal came up and said, "Everything all right? Did you get the job, huh?" I said, "Yeah, thanks an awful lot." He said, "That's all right. Listen, do a good job. I mean, if it's commercial, play commercial. What the hell! I mean, if you don't then it's my ass, you know. It isn't even only my ass, it's Tony's and that other guy's, it's about four different asses, you know."

In short, to get these top job positions requires both ability and the formation of informal relationships of mutual obligation with men who can sponsor one for the jobs. Without the necessary minimum of ability one cannot perform successfully at the new level, but this ability will command the appropriate kind of work only if a man has made the proper connections. For sponsors, as the above quotation indicates, the system operates to bring available men to the attention of those who have jobs to fill and to provide them with recruits who can be trusted to perform adequately.

The successful career may be viewed as a series of such steps, each one a sequence of sponsorship, successful performance, and the building up of relationships at each new level.

I have noted a similarity between the musician's career and careers in medicine and industry, shown in the fact that successful functioning and professional mobility are functions of the individual's relation to a network of informal organizations composed of his colleagues. I turn now to the variation in this typical social form created by the strong emphasis of musicians on maintaining their freedom to play without interference from nonmusicians, who are felt to lack understanding and appreciation of the musician's mysterious, artistic gifts. Since it is difficult (if not impossible) to attain this desired freedom, most men find it necessary to sacrifice the standards of their profession to some degree in order to meet the demands of audiences and of those who control employment opportunities. This creates another dimension of professional prestige, based on the degree to which one refuses to modify one's performance in deference to outside demands—from the one extreme of "playing what you feel" to the other of "playing what the people want to hear." The jazzman plays what he feels while the commercial musician caters to public taste; the commercial viewpoint is best summarized in a statement attributed to a very successful commercial musician: "I'll do anything for a dollar."

As I pointed out earlier, musicians feel that there is a conflict inherent in this situation, that one cannot please the audience and at the same time maintain one's artistic integrity. The following quotation, from an interview with a radio staff musician, illustrates the kind of pressures in the top jobs that produce such conflict:

The big thing down at the studio is not to make any mistakes. You see, they don't care whether you play a thing well or not, as long as you play all the notes and don't make any mistakes. Of course, you care if it doesn't sound good, but they're not interested in that. . . . They don't care what you sound like when you go through that mike, all they care about is the commercial. I mean, you might have some personal pride about it, but they don't care. . . . That's what you have to do. Give him what you know he likes already.

The job with most prestige is thus one in which the musician must sacrifice his artistic independence and the concomitant prestige in professional terms. A very successful commercial musician paid deference to artistic independence while stressing its negative effect on career development:

I know, you probably like to play jazz. Sure I understand. I used to be interested in jazz, but I found out that didn't pay, people didn't like jazz. They like rumbas. After all, this is a business, ain't that right? You're in it to make a living or you're not, that's all. And if you want to make a living you can't throw jazz at the people all the time, they won't take it. So you have to play what they want, they're the ones that are paying the bills. I mean, don't get me wrong. Any guy that can make a living playing jazz, fine. But I'd like to see the guy that can do it. If you want to get anywhere you gotta be commercial.

Jazzmen, on the other hand, complain of the low position of the jobs available to them in terms of income and things other than artistic prestige.

Thus the cliques to which one must gain access if one is to achieve job success and security are made up of men who are definitely commercial in their orientation. The greatest rewards of the profession are controlled by men who have sacrificed some of the most basic professional standards, and one must make a similar sacrifice in order to have any chance of moving into the desirable positions:

See, if you play commercial like that, you can get in with these cliques that have all the good jobs and you can really do well. I've played some of the best jobs in town—the Q—— Club and places like that—and that's the way you have to do. Play that way and get in with these guys, then you never have to worry. You can count on making that gold every week and that's what counts.

Cliques made up of jazzmen offer their members nothing but the prestige of maintaining artistic integrity; commercial cliques offer security, mobility, income, and general social prestige.

This conflict is a major problem in the career of the individual musician, and the development of his career is contingent on his reaction to it. Although I gathered no data on the point, it seems reasonable to assume that most men enter music with a great respect for jazz and artistic freedom. At a certain point in the development of the career (which varies from individual to individual), the conflict becomes apparent and the musician realizes that it is impossible to achieve the kind of success he desires and maintain independence of musical performance. When the incompatibility of these goals becomes obvious, some sort of choice must be made, if only by default, thus determining the further course of his career.

One response to the dilemma is to avoid it, by leaving the profession. Unable to find a satisfactory resolution of the problem, the individual cuts his career off. The rationale of such a move is disclosed in the following statement by one who had made it:

It's better to take a job you know you're going to be dragged [depressed] with, where you expect to be dragged, than one in music, where it could be great but isn't. Like you go into business, you don't know anything about it. So you figure it's going to be a drag and you expect it. But music can be so great that it's a big drag when it isn't. So it's better to have some other kind of job that won't drag you that way.

We have seen the range of responses to this dilemma on the part of those who remain in the profession. The jazzman ignores audience demands for artistic standards while the commercial musician does the opposite, both feeling the pressure of these two forces. My concern here will be to discuss the relation of these responses to career fates.

The man who chooses to ignore commercial pressures finds himself effectively barred from moving up to jobs of greater prestige and income, and from membership in those cliques which would provide him with security and the opportunity for such mobility. Few men are willing or able to take such an extreme position; most compromise to some degree. The pattern of movement involved in this compromise is a common career phenomenon, well known among musicians and assumed to be practically inevitable:

I saw K—— E——. I said, "Get me a few jobbing dates, will you?" He said, imitating one of the "old guys," [6] "Now son, when you get wise and commercial, I'll be able to help you out, but not now." In his normal voice he continued, "Why don't you get with it? Gosh, I'm leading the trend over to commercialism, I guess. I certainly have gone in for it in a big way, haven't I?"

At this crucial point in his career the individual finds it necessary to make a radical change in his self-conception; he must learn to think of himself in a new way, to regard himself as a different kind of person:

This commercial business has really gotten me, I guess. You know, even when I go on a job where you're supposed to blow

6. "Old guys" was the term generally used by younger men to refer to the cliques controlling the most desirable jobs.

jazz, where you can just let yourself go and play anything, I think about being commercial, about playing what the people out there might want to hear. I used to go on a job with the idea to play the best I could, that's all, just play the best I knew how. And now I go on a job and I just automatically think, "What will these people want to hear? Do they want to hear Kenton style, or like Dizzy Gillespie [jazz orchestras], or like Guy Lombardo [a commercial orchestra], or what?" I can't help thinking that to myself. They've really gotten it into me, I guess they've broken my spirit.

A more drastic change of self-conception related to this career dilemma is found in this statement:

I'll tell you, I've decided the only thing to do is really go commercial—play what the people want to hear. I think there's a good place for the guy that'll give them just what they want. The melody, that's all. No improvising, no technical stuff—just the plain melody. I'll tell you, why shouldn't I play that way? After all, let's quit kidding ourselves. Most of us aren't really musicians, we're just instrumentalists. I mean, I think of myself as something like a common laborer, you know. No sense trying to fool myself. Most of those guys are just instrumentalists, they're not real musicians at all, they should stop trying to kid themselves they are.

Making such a decision and undergoing such a change in self-conception open the way for movement into the upper levels of the job hierarchy and create the conditions in which complete success is possible, if one can follow up the opportunity by making and maintaining the proper connections.

One way of adjusting to the realities of the job without sacrificing self-respect is to adopt the orientation of the craftsman. The musician who does this no longer concerns himself with the *kind* of music he plays. Instead, he is interested only in whether it is played *correctly*, in whether he has the skills necessary to do the job the way it ought to be done. He finds his pride and self-respect in being able to "cut" any kind of music, in always giving an adequate performance.

The skills necessary to maintain this orientation vary with the setting in which the musician performs. The man who works in bars with small groups will pride himself on knowing hundreds (or even thousands) of songs and being able to play them in any key. The man who works with a big band will pride himself on his intonation and technical virtuosity. The man who works in a night club or radio studio boasts of his ability to read any kind of music accurately and precisely at sight. This kind of orientation, since it is likely to produce just what the employer wants and at a superior level of quality, is likely to lead to occupational success.

The craftsman orientation is easier to sustain in the major musical centers of the country: Chicago, New York, Los Angeles. In these cities, the volume of available work is great enough to support specialization, and a man can devote himself single-mindedly to improving one set of skills. One finds musicians of astounding virtuosity in these centers. In smaller cities, in contrast, there is not enough work of any one kind for a man to specialize, and musicians are called on to do a little of everything. Although the necessary skills overlap—intonation, for instance, is always important—every man has areas in which he is just barely competent. A trumpet player may play excellent jazz and do well on small jazz jobs but read poorly and do much less well when he works with a big band. It is difficult to maintain pride as a craftsman when one is continually faced with jobs for which he has only minimal skills.

To sum up, the emphasis of musicians on freedom from the interference inevitable in their work creates a new dimension of professional prestige which conflicts with the previously discussed job prestige in such a way that one cannot rank high in both. The greatest rewards are in the hands of those who have sacrificed their artistic independence, and who demand a similar sacrifice from those they recruit for these higher positions. This creates a dilemma for the individual musician, and his response determines the future course of his career. Refusing to submit means that all hope of achieving jobs of high prestige and income must be abandoned, while giving in to commercial pressures opens the way to success for them. (Studies of other occupations might devote attention to those career contingencies which are, likewise, a function of the occupation's basic work problems vis-à-vis clients or customers.)

Parents and Wives

I have noted that musicians extend their desire for freedom from outside interference in their work to a generalized feeling that they should not be bound by the ordinary conventions of their society. The ethos of the profession fosters an admiration for spontaneous and individualistic behavior and a disregard for the rules of society in general. We may expect that members of an occupation with such an ethos will have problems of conflict when they come into close contact with that society. One point of contact is on the job, where the audience is the source of trouble. The effect of this area of problems on the career has been described above.

Another area of contact between profession and society is the family. Membership in families binds the musician to people who are squares, outsiders who abide by social conventions whose authority the musician does not acknowledge. Such relationships bear seeds of conflict which can break out with disastrous consequences for the career and/or the family tie.

This section will spell out the nature of these conflicts and their effect on the career.

The individual's family has a great influence on his occupational choice through its power to sponsor and aid the neophyte in his chosen career. Hall, in his discussion of the early stages of the medical career, notes that:

In most cases family or friends played a significant role by envisaging the career line and reinforcing the efforts of the recruit. They accomplished the latter by giving encouragement, helping establish the appropriate routines, arranging the necessary privacy, discouraging anomalous behavior, and defining the day-to-day rewards.[7]

The musician's parents ordinarily do not aid the development of his career in this way. On the contrary, as one man observed, "My God, most guys have had a terrific hassle with their parents about going into the music business." The reason is clear: regardless of the social class from which he comes, it is usually obvious to the prospective musician's family that he is entering a profession which encourages his breaking with the conventional behavior patterns of his family's social milieu. Lower-class families seem to have been most distressed over the irregularity of musical employment, although there is evidence that some families encouraged such a career, seeing it as a possible mobility route. In the middle-class family, choice of dance music as an occupation is viewed as a movement into Bohemianism, involving a possible loss of prestige for both individual and family, and is vigorously opposed. Considerable pressure is applied to the person to give up his choice:

7. Hall, *op. cit.*, p. 328. See also Becker, "The Implications of Research on Occupational Careers . . . ," *op. cit.*; and James W. Carper and Howard S. Becker, "Adjustments to Conflicting Expectations in the Development of Identification with an Occupation," *Social Forces*, 36 (October, 1957), 51–56.

You know, everybody thought it was pretty terrible when I decided to be a musician. . . . I remember I graduated from high school on a Thursday and left town on Monday for a job. Here my parents were arguing with me and all my relatives, too, they were really giving me a hard time. . . . This one uncle of mine came on so strong about how it wasn't a regular life and how could I ever get married and all that stuff.

The conflict has two typical effects on the career. First, the prospective musician may, in the face of family pressure, give up music as a profession. Such an adjustment is fairly common at an early stage of the career. On the other hand, the young musician may ignore his family's desires and continue his career, in which case he is often deprived of his family's support at an earlier age than would otherwise be the case and must begin to "go it alone," making his way without the family sponsorship and financial aid that might otherwise be forthcoming. In music, then, the career is ordinarily begun, if at all, without the family aid and encouragement typical of careers in many other occupations.

Once he has married and established his own family, the musician has entered a relationship in which the conventions of society are presented to him in an immediate and forceful way. As a husband he is expected by his wife, typically a non-musician, to be a companion and provider. In some occupations there is no conflict between the demands of work and of the family. In others there is conflict, but socially-sanctioned resolutions of it exist which are accepted by both partners as, for example, in medical practice. In deviant occupations, such as the music business, professional expectations do not mesh at all with lay expectations, with consequent difficulties for the musician.

Musicians feel that the imperatives of their work must take

precedence over those of their families, and they act accordingly:

Man, my wife's a great chick, but there's no way for us to stay together, not as long as I'm in the music business. No way, no way at all. When we first got married it was great. I was working in town, making good gold, everybody was happy. But when that job was through, I didn't have anything. Then I got an offer to go on the road. Well, hell, I needed the money, I took it. Sally said, "No, I want you here in town, with me." She'd sooner have had me go to work in a factory! Well, that's a bunch of crap. So I just left with the band. Hell, I like the business too much, I'm not gonna put it down for her or any woman.

Marriage is likely to turn into a continuing struggle over this issue; the outcome of the struggle determines whether the man's musical career will be cut short or will continue, as the following incident from my field notes illustrates:

The boys down at the Z—— Club are trying to get Jay Marlowe to go back to work there full time. He's splitting the week with someone now. He's got a day job in the same office in which his wife works, doing bookkeeping or some minor clerical job. The boys are trying to talk him into quitting. Apparently his wife is bitterly opposed to this.

Jay's been a musician all his life, as far as I know; probably the first time he ever had a day job. Gene, the drummer at the Z—— Club, said to me, "It's foolish for him to have a day job. How much can he make down there? Probably doesn't clear more than thirty, thirty-five a week. He makes that much in three nights here. Course, his wife wanted him to get out of the business. She didn't like the idea of all those late hours and the chicks that hang around bars, that kind of stuff. But after all, when a guy can do something and make more money, why should he take a sad job and work for peanuts? It don't make sense. Besides, why should he drag himself? He'd rather be playing and it's a drag to him to have that fucking day job, so why should he hold on to it?" Johnny, the saxophone player, said, "You know why, because his wife makes him hold on to it." Gene said, "He shouldn't let her boss him around like that. For Christ Sake, my old lady don't tell me what to do. He shouldn't put up with that crap."

They've started to do something about it. They've been inviting Jay to go out to the race track with them on week days and he's been skipping work to do so. Gene, after one of these occasions, said, "Boy was his wife mad! She doesn't want him to goof off and lose that job, and she knows what we're up to. She thinks we're bad influences. Well, I guess we are, from her way of thinking."

[A few weeks later Marlowe quit his day job and returned to music.]

For other men who feel their family responsibilities more strongly the situation is not so simple. The economic insecurity of the music business makes it difficult to be a good provider, and may force the individual to leave the profession, one of the typical patterns of response to this situation:

No, I haven't been working too much. I think I'm going to get a Goddamn day job. You know, when you're married it's a little different. Before it was different. I worked, I didn't work, all the same thing. If I needed money I'd borrow five from my mother. Now those bills just won't wait. When you're married you got to keep working or else you just can't make it.

Even if the career is not cut off in this fashion, the demands of marriage exert a very strong pressure that pushes the musician toward going commercial:

If you want to keep on working, you have to put up with some crap once in a while. . . . I don't care. I've got a wife and I want to keep working. If some square comes up and asks me to play the "Beer Barrel Polka" I just smile and play it.

Marriage can thus speed the achievement of success by forcing a decision which affords, although it does not guarantee, the opportunity for movement into those cliques which, being commercially oriented, are best able to keep their members in steady work.

The family then, as an institution that demands that the musician behave conventionally, creates problems for him of conflicting pressures, loyalties and self-conceptions. His response to these problems has a decisive effect on the duration and direction of his career.

7 Rules and Their Enforcement

WE have considered some general characteristics of deviants and the processes by which they are labeled outsiders and come to view themselves as outsiders. We have looked at the cultures and typical career patterns of two outsider groups: marihuana users and dance musicians. It is now time to consider the other half of the equation: the people who make and enforce the rules to which outsiders fail to conform.

The question here is simply: when are rules made and enforced? I noted earlier that the existence of a rule does not automatically guarantee that it will be enforced. There are many variations in rule enforcement. We cannot account for rule enforcement by invoking some abstract group that is ever vigilant; we cannot say that "society" is harmed by every infraction and acts to restore the balance. We might posit, as one extreme, a group in which this was the case, in which all rules were absolutely and automatically enforced. But imagining such an extreme case only serves to make more clear the fact that social groups are ordinarily not like this. It is more typical for rules to be enforced only when something provokes enforcement. Enforcement, then, requires explanation.

The explanation rests on several premises. First, enforcement of a rule is an enterprising act. Someone—an entrepreneur—must take the initiative in punishing the culprit. Second, enforcement occurs when those who want the rule enforced publicly bring the infraction to the attention of others; an infraction cannot be ignored once it is made public. Put another way, enforcement occurs when someone blows the whistle. Third, people blow the whistle, making enforcement necessary, when they see some advantage in doing so. Personal interest prods them to take the initiative. Finally, the kind of personal interest that prompts enforcement varies with the complexity of the situation in which enforcement takes place. Let us consider several cases, noting the way personal interest, enterprise, and publicity interact with the complexity of the situation to produce both rule enforcement and the failure to enforce rules.

Recall Malinowski's example of the Trobriand Islander who had committed clan incest. Everyone knew what he was doing, but no one did anything about it. Then the girl's former lover, who had intended to marry her and thus felt personally aggrieved by her choice of another man, took matters into his own hands and publicly accused Kima'i of incest. In doing this he changed the situation so that Kima'i had no choice but to commit suicide. Here, in a society of relatively simple structure, there is no conflict over the rule; everyone agrees that clan incest is wrong. Once personal interest evokes someone's initiative, he can guarantee enforcement by making the infraction public.

We find a similar lack of conflict over rule enforcement in the less organized situations of anonymous urban life. But the consequence is different, for the substance of people's agreement is that they will not call attention to or interfere in even the grossest violations of law. The city dweller minds his own business and does nothing about rule infractions unless it is his own business that is being interfered with. Simmel labeled the typical urban attitude "reserve":

If so many inner reactions were responses to the continuous external contacts with innumerable people as are those in the small town, where one knows almost everybody one meets and where one has a positive relation to almost everyone, one would be completely atomized internally and come to an unimaginable psychic state. Partly this psychological fact, partly the right to distrust which men have in the face of the touch-and-go elements of metropolitan life, necessitates our reserve. As a result of this reserve we frequently do not even know by sight those who have been our neighbors for years. And it is this reserve which in the eyes of the small-town people makes us appear to be cold and heartless. Indeed, if I do not deceive myself, the inner aspect of this outer reserve is not only indifference but, more often than we are aware, it is a slight aversion, a mutual strangeness and repulsion, which will break into hatred and fright at the moment of a closer contact, however caused. . . .

This reserve with its overtone of hidden aversion appears in turn as the form or the cloak of a more general mental phenomenon of the metropolis: it grants to the individual a kind and an amount of personal freedom which has no analogy whatsoever under other conditions.[1]

1. Kurt H. Wolff, translator and editor, *The Sociology of Georg Simmel* (New York: The Free Press of Glencoe, 1950), pp. 415–416.

Several years ago, a national magazine published a series of pictures illustrating urban reserve. A man lay unconscious on a busy city street. Picture after picture showed pedestrians either ignoring his existence or noticing him and then turning aside to go about their business.

Reserve, while typically found in cities, is not characteristic of all urban life. Many urban areas—some slums and sections which are ethnically homogeneous—have something of the character of a small town; their inhabitants see everything that goes on in the neighborhood as their business. The urbanite displays his reserve most markedly in anonymous public areas —the Times Squares and State Streets—where he can feel that nothing that goes on is his responsibility and that there are professional law enforcers present whose job it is to deal with anything out of the ordinary. The agreement to ignore rule infractions rests in part on the knowledge that enforcement can be left to these professionals.

In more complexly structured situations, there is greater possibility of differing interpretations of the situation and possible conflict over the enforcement of rules. Where an organization contains two groups competing for power—as in industry, where managers and employees vie for control over the work situation—conflict may be chronic. Yet, precisely because the conflict is a persistent feature of the organization, it may never become open. Instead, the two groups, enmeshed in a situation that constrains both of them, see an advantage in allowing each other to commit certain infractions and do not blow the whistle.

Melville Dalton has studied systematic rule-breaking by employees of industrial organizations, department stores, and similar work establishments. He reports that employees frequently appropriate services and materials belonging to the organization for their own personal use, noting that this would ordinarily be regarded as theft. Management tries to stop this diversion of resources, but is seldom successful. They do not, however, ordinarily bring the matter to public attention. Among the examples of misappropriation of company resources Dalton cites are the following:

A foreman built a machine shop in his home, equipping it with expensive machinery taken from the shop in which he worked. The loot included a drill press, shaper, lathe and cutters and drills, bench equipment, and a grinding machine.

The foreman of the carpenter shop in a large factory, a European-born craftsman, spent most of his workday building household objects—baby beds, storm windows, tables, and similar custom-made items—for higher executives. In return, he received gifts of wine and dressed fowl.

An office worker did all her letter writing on the job, using company materials and stamps.

An X-ray technician in a hospital stole hams and canned food from the hospital and felt he was entitled to do so because of his low salary.

A retired industrial executive had an eleven unit aviary built in factory shops and installed in his home by factory personnel. Plant carpenters repaired and reconditioned the bird houses each spring.

Additions to the buildings of a local yacht club, many of whose members worked in the affected factories, were made by company workers on company time with company materials.

Heads of clothing departments in department stores marked goods they wanted for their personal use "damaged" and lowered the price accordingly. They also sold sale items above the sale price in order to accumulate a fund of money against which their appropriation of items for personal use could be charged.[2]

2. Melville Dalton, *Men Who Manage: Fusions of Feeling and Theory in Administration* (New York: John Wiley and Sons, 1959), pp. 199–205.

Dalton says that to call all these actions theft is to miss the point. In fact, he insists, management, even while officially condemning intramural theft, conspires in it; it is not a system of theft at all, but a system of rewards. People who appropriate services and materials belonging to the organization are really being rewarded unofficially for extraordinary contributions they make to the operation of the organization for which no legitimate system of rewards exists. The foreman who equipped his home machine shop from factory supplies was in fact being rewarded for giving up Catholicism and becoming a Mason in order to demonstrate his fitness for a supervisory position. The X-ray technician was allowed to steal food from the hospital because the hospital administration knew it was not paying him a salary sufficient to command his loyalty and hard work.[3] The rules are not enforced because two competing power groups—management and workers—find mutual advantage in ignoring infractions.

Donald Roy has described similar evasions of rules in a machine shop, showing again that one group will not blow the whistle on another if they are both partners in a system characterized by a balance of power and interest. The machine operators Roy studied were paid by the piece, and rule-breaking occurred when they tried to "make out"—earn far more than their hourly base pay on given piece-work jobs. Frequently they could make out only by cutting corners and doing the job in a way forbidden by company rules (ignoring safety precautions or using tools and techniques not allowed in the job specifications).[4] Roy describes a "shop syndicate," which cooperated with machine operators in evading formally

3. *Ibid.*, pp. 194–215.
4. Donald Roy, "Quota Restriction and Goldbricking in a Machine Shop," *American Journal of Sociology*, LVII (March, 1952), 427–442.

established shop routines.[5] Inspectors, tool-crib men, time-checkers, stock men, and set-up men all participated in helping the machinists make out.

For instance, machine operators were not supposed to keep tools at their machines that were not being used for the job they were then working on. Roy shows how, when this new rule was promulgated, tool-crib attendents first obeyed it. But they found that it led to a continually present crowd around the tool-crib window, a group of complaining men who made the attendant's workday difficult. Consequently, shortly after the rule was first announced, attendants began breaking it, letting men keep tools at their machine or wander in and out of the tool-crib as they pleased. By allowing the machinists to break the rule, tool-crib attendants eased their own situation; they were no longer annoyed by the complaints of disgruntled operators.

The problem of rule enforcement becomes more complicated when the situation contains several competing groups. Accommodation and compromise are more difficult, because there are more interests to be served, and conflict is more likely to be open and unresolved. Under these circumstances, access to the channels of publicity becomes an important variable, and those whose interest demands that rules not be enforced try to prevent news of infractions.

An apt example can be found in the role of the public prosecutor. One of his jobs is to supervise grand juries. Grand juries are convened to hear evidence and decide whether indictments should be returned against individuals said to have broken the law. Although they ordinarily confine themselves

5. Donald Roy, "Efficiency and 'The Fix': Informal Intergroup Relations in a Piecework Machine Shop," *American Journal of Sociology*, LX (November, 1954), 255–266.

to cases the prosecutor presents to them, grand juries have the power to make investigations on their own and return indictments that have not been suggested by the prosecutor. Conscious of its mandate to protect the public interest, a grand jury may feel the prosecutor is hiding things from it.

And, indeed, the prosecutor may be hiding something. He may be a party to agreements made between politicians, police, and criminals to allow vice, gambling, and other forms of crime to operate; even if he is not directly involved, he may have political obligations to those who are. It is difficult to find a workable compromise between the interests of crime and corrupt politics and those of a grand jury determined to do its job, more difficult than it is to find satisfactory compromises between two power groups operating in the same factory.

The corrupt prosecutor, faced with this dilemma, attempts to play on the jury's ignorance of legal procedure. But occasionally one hears of a "runaway" grand jury, one which has overcome the prosecutor's resistance and begun to investigate those matters he wants it to stay away from. Exhibiting enterprise and generating embarrassing publicity, the runaway jury exposes infractions heretofore kept from public view and often provokes a widespread drive against corruption of all kinds. The existence of runaway grand juries reminds us that the function of the corrupt prosecutor is precisely to prevent them from occurring.

Enterprise, generated by personal interest, armed with publicity, and conditioned by the character of the organization, is thus the key variable in rule enforcement. Enterprise operates most immediately in a situation in which there is fundamental agreement on the rules to be enforced. A person with an interest to be served publicizes an infraction and action is taken; if no enterprising person appears, no action is taken. When two competing power groups exist in the same organization, enforcement will occur only when the systems of compromise that characterize their relationship break down; otherwise, everyone's interest is best served by allowing infractions to continue. In situations containing many competing interest groups, the outcome is variable, depending on the relative power of the groups involved and their access to channels of publicity. We will see the play of all these factors in a complex situation when we examine the history of the Marihuana Tax Act.

Stages of Enforcement

Before looking at that history, however, let us consider the problem of rule enforcement from another perspective. We have seen how the process by which rules are enforced varies in different kinds of social structures. Let us now add the dimension of time, and look briefly at the various stages through which enforcement of a rule goes—its natural history.

Natural history differs from history in being concerned with what is generic to a class of phenomena rather than what is unique in each instance. It seeks to discover what is typical of a class of events rather than what makes them differ— regularity rather than idiosyncrasy. Thus I will be concerned here with those features of the process by which rules are made and enforced that are generic to that process and constitute its distinctive insignia.

In considering the stages in the development of a rule and its enforcement, I will use a legal model. This should not be taken to mean that what I have to say applies only to legislation. The same processes occur in the development and enforcement of less formally constituted rules as well.

Specific rules find their beginnings in those vague and generalized statements of preference social scientists often call values. Scholars have proposed many varying definitions of value, but we need not enter that controversy here. The definition proposed by Talcott Parsons will serve as well as any:

An element of a shared symbolic system which serves as a criterion or standard for selection among the alternatives of orientation which are intrinsically open in a situation may be called a value.[6]

Equality, for example, is an American value. We prefer to treat people equally, without reference to the differences among them, when we can. Freedom of the individual is also an American value. We prefer to allow people to do what they wish, unless there are strong reasons to the contrary.

Values, however, are poor guides to action. The standards of selection they embody are general, telling us which of several alternative lines of action would be preferable, all other things being equal. But all other things are seldom equal in the concrete situations of everyday life. We find it difficult to relate the generalities of a value statement to the complex and specific details of everyday situations. We cannot easily and unambiguously relate the vague notion of equality to the concrete reality, so that it is hard to know what specific line of action the value would recommend in a given situation.

Another difficulty in using values as a guide to action lies in the fact that, because they are so vague and general, it is possible for us to hold conflicting values without being aware of the conflict. We become aware of their inadequacy as a basis for action when, in a moment of crisis, we realize that we cannot decide which of the conflicting courses of action recommended to us we should take. Thus, to take a specific

6. Talcott Parsons, *The Social System* (New York: The Free Press of Glencoe, 1951), p. 12.

example, we espouse the value of equality and this leads us to forbid racial segregation. But we also espouse the value of individual freedom, which inhibits us from interfering with people who practice segregation in their private lives. When a Negro who owns a sailboat announces, as one recently did, that no yacht club in the New York area will admit him as a member, we find that our values cannot help us decide what ought to be done about it. (Conflict also arises between specific rules, as when a state law forbids racial integration in public schools and Federal law demands it. But here determinate judicial procedures exist for resolving the conflict.)

Since values can furnish only a general guide to action and are not useful in deciding on courses of action in concrete situations, people develop specific rules more closely tied to the realities of everyday life. Values provide the major premises from which specific rules are deduced.

People shape values into specific rules in problematic situations. They perceive some area of their existence as troublesome or difficult, requiring action.[7] After considering the various values to which they subscribe, they select one or more of them as relevant to their difficulties and deduce from it a specific rule. The rule, framed to be consistent with the value, states with relative precision which actions are approved and which forbidden, the situations to which the rule is applicable, and the sanctions attached to breaking it.

The ideal type of a specific rule is a piece of carefully drawn legislation, well encrusted with judicial interpretation. Such a rule is not ambiguous. On the contrary, its provisions are precise; one knows quite accurately what he can and cannot do and what will happen if he does the wrong thing.

7. For a natural history approach to social problems, see Richard C. Fuller and R. R. Meyers, "Some Aspects of a Theory of Social Problems," *American Sociological Review*, 6 (February, 1941), 24–32.

(This is an ideal type. Most rules are not so precise and fool-proof; though they are far less ambiguous than values, they too may cause us difficulty in deciding on courses of action.)

Just because values are ambiguous and general, we can interpret them in various ways and deduce many kinds of rules from them. A rule may be consistent with a given value, but widely differing rules might also have been deduced from the same value. Furthermore, rules will not be deduced from values unless a problematic situation prompts someone to make the deduction. We may find that certain rules which seem to us to flow logically from a widely held value have not even been thought of by the people who hold the value, either because situations and problems calling for the rule have not arisen or because they are unaware that a problem exists. Again, a specific rule, if deduced from the general value, might conflict with other rules deduced from other values. The conflict, whether consciously known or only recognized implictly, may inhibit the creation of a particular rule. Rules do not flow automatically from values.

Because a rule may satisfy one interest and yet conflict with other interests of the group making it, care is usually taken in framing a rule to insure that it will accomplish only what it is supposed to and no more. Specific rules are fenced in with qualifications and exceptions, so that they will not interfere with values we deem important. The laws of obscenity are an example. The general intent of such laws is that matters which are morally repugnant shall not be broadcast publicly. But this conflicts with another important value, the value of free speech. In addition, it conflicts with the commercial and career interests of authors, playwrights, publishers, booksellers, and theatrical producers. Various adjustments and qualifications have been made so that the law as it now stands lacks the broad scope desired by those who deeply believe obscenity to be a harmful thing.

Specific rules may be embodied in legislation. They may simply be customary in a particular group, armed only with informal sanctions. Legal rules, naturally, are most likely to be precise and unambiguous; informal and customary rules are most likely to be vague and to have large areas in which various interpretations of them can be made.

But the natural history of a rule does not end with the deduction of a specific rule from a general value. The specific rule has still to be applied in particular instances to particular people. It must receive its final embodiment in particular acts of enforcement.

We have seen in an earlier chapter that acts of enforcement do not follow automatically on the infraction of a rule. Enforcement is selective, and selective differentially among kinds of people, at different times, and in different situations.

We can question whether all rules follow the sequence from general value through specific rule to particular act of enforcement. Values may contain an unused potential—rules not yet deduced which can, under the proper circumstances, grow into full-fledged specific rules. Similarly, many specific rules are never enforced. On the other hand, are there any rules which do not have their base in some general value? Or acts of enforcement which do not find their justification in some particular rule? Many rules, of course, are quite technical and may really be said to have their base, not in some general value, but rather in an effort to make peace between other and earlier rules. The specific rules governing securities transactions, for instance, are probably of this type. They do not seem so much an effort to implement a general value as an effort to regularize the workings of a complex institution. Similarly, we may find individual acts of enforcement based on rules invented at the moment solely to justify the act. Some of the informal and extralegal activities of policemen fall in this category.

If we recognize these instances as deviations from the natural history model, to how many of the things we might be interested in does the model actually apply? This is a question of fact, to be settled by research on various kinds of rules in various situations. At the least, we know that many rules go through this sequence. Furthermore, when the sequence is not followed originally, it is often filled in retroactively. That is, a rule may be drawn up simply to serve someone's special interest and a rationale for it later found in some general value. In the same way, a spontaneous act of enforcement may be legitimized by creating a rule to which it can be related. In these cases, the formal relation of general to specific is preserved, even though the time sequence has been altered.

If many rules get their form by moving through a sequence from general value to specific act of enforcement but movement through the sequence is not automatic or inevitable, we must, to account for steps in this sequence, focus on the entrepreneur, who sees to it that the movement takes place. If general values are made the basis for specific rules deduced from them, we must look for the person who made it his business to see that the rules were deduced. And if specific rules are applied to specific people in specific circumstances, we must look to see who it is that has made it his business to see that application and enforcement of the rules takes place. We will be concerned, then, with the entrepreneur, the circumstances in which he appears, and how he applies his enterprising instincts.

An Illustrative Case: The Marihuana Tax Act

It is generally assumed that the practice of smoking marihuana was imported into the United States from Mexico, by way of the southwestern states of Arizona, New Mexico, and Texas, all of which had sizable Spanish-speaking populations. People first began to notice marihuana use in the nineteen-twenties but, since it was a new phenomenon and one apparently confined to Mexican immigrants, did not express much concern about it. (The medical compound prepared from the marihuana plant had been known for some time, but was not often prescribed by U.S. physicians.) As late as 1930, only sixteen states had passed laws prohibiting the use of marihuana.

In 1937, however, the United States Congress passed the Marihuana Tax Act, designed to stamp out use of the drug. According to the theory outlined above, we should find in the history of this Act the story of an entrepreneur whose initiative and enterprise overcame public apathy and indifference and culminated in the passage of Federal legislation. Before turning to the history of the Act itself, we should perhaps look at the way similar substances had been treated in American law, in order to understand the context in which the attempt to suppress marihuana use proceeded.

The use of alcohol and opium in the United States had a long history, punctuated by attempts at suppression.[8] Three

8. See John Krout, *The Origins of Prohibition* (New York: Columbia University Press, 1928); Charles Terry and Mildred Pellens, *The Opium Problem* (New York: The Committee on Drug Addiction with the Bureau of Social Hygiene, Inc., 1928); and *Drug Addiction: Crime or Disease?* Interim and Final Reports of the Joint Committee of the American Bar Association and the American Medical Association on Narcotic Drugs (Bloomington, Indiana: Indiana University Press, 1961).

values provided legitimacy for attempts to prevent the use of intoxicants and narcotics. One legitimizing value, a component of what has been called the Protestant Ethic, holds that the individual should exercise complete responsibility for what he does and what happens to him; he should never do anything that might cause loss of self-control. Alcohol and the opiate drugs, in varying degrees and ways, cause people to lose control of themselves; their use, therefore, is evil. A person intoxicated with alcohol often loses control over his physical activity; the centers of judgment in the brain are also affected. Users of opiates are more likely to be anesthetized and thus less likely to commit rash acts. But they become dependent on the drug to prevent withdrawal symptoms and in this sense have lost control of their actions; insofar as it is difficult to obtain the drug, they must subordinate other interests to its pursuit.

Another American value legitimized attempts to suppress the use of alcohol and opiates: disapproval of action taken solely to achieve states of ecstasy. Perhaps because of our strong cultural emphases on pragmatism and utilitarianism, Americans usually feel uneasy and ambivalent about ecstatic experiences of any kind. But we do not condemn ecstatic experience when it is the by-product or reward of actions we consider proper in their own right, such as hard work or religious fervor. It is only when people pursue ecstasy for its own sake that we condemn their action as a search for "illicit pleasure," an expression that has real meaning to us.

The third value which provided a basis for attempts at suppression was humanitarianism. Reformers believed that people enslaved by the use of alcohol and opium would benefit from laws making it impossible for them to give in to their weaknesses. The families of drunkards and drug addicts would likewise benefit.

These values provided the basis for specific rules. The

Eighteenth Amendment and the Volstead Act forbade the importation of alcoholic beverages into the United States and their manufacture within the country. The Harrison Act in effect prohibited the use of opiate drugs for all but medical purposes.

In formulating these laws, care was taken not to interfere with what were regarded as the legitimate interests of other groups in the society. The Harrison Act, for instance, was so drawn as to allow medical personnel to continue using morphine and other opium derivatives for the relief of pain and such other medical purposes as seemed to them appropriate. Furthermore, the law was carefully drawn in order to avoid running afoul of the constitutional provision reserving police powers to the several states. In line with this restriction, the Act was presented as a revenue measure, taxing unlicensed purveyors of opiate drugs at an exorbitant rate while permitting licensed purveyors (primarily physicians, dentists, veterinarians, and pharmacists) to pay a nominal tax. Though it was justified constitutionally as a revenue measure, the Harrison Act was in fact a police measure and was so interpreted by those to whom its enforcement was entrusted. One consequence of the passage of the Act was the establishment, in the Treasury Department, of the Federal Bureau of Narcotics in 1930.

The same values that led to the banning of the use of alcohol and opiates could, of course, be applied to the case of marihuana and it seems logical that this should have been done. Yet what little I have been told, by people familiar with the period, about the use of marihuana in the late 'twenties and early 'thirties leads me to believe that there was relatively lax enforcement of the existing local laws. This, after all, was the era of Prohibition and the police had more pressing matters to attend to. Neither the public nor law enforcement officers, apparently, considered the use of marihuana a serious problem. When they noticed it at all, they probably dismissed it as not warranting major attempts at enforcement. One index of how feebly the laws were enforced is that the price of marihuana is said to have been very much lower prior to the passage of Federal legislation. This indicates that there was little danger in selling it and that enforcement was not seriously undertaken.

Even the Treasury Department, in its report on the year 1931, minimized the importance of the problem:

A great deal of public interest has been aroused by newspaper articles appearing from time to time on the evils of the abuse of marihuana, or Indian hemp, and more attention has been focused on specific cases reported of the abuse of the drug than would otherwise have been the case. This publicity tends to magnify the extent of the evil and lends color to an inference that there is an alarming spread of the improper use of the drug, whereas the actual increase in such use may not have been inordinately large.[9]

The Treasury Department's Bureau of Narcotics furnished most of the enterprise that produced the Marihuana Tax Act. While it is, of course, difficult to know what the motives of Bureau officials were, we need assume no more than that they perceived an area of wrongdoing that properly belonged in their jurisdiction and moved to put it there. The personal interest they satisfied in pressing for marihuana legislation was one common to many officials: the interest in successfully accomplishing the task one has been assigned and in acquiring the best tools with which to accomplish it. The Bureau's efforts took two forms: cooperating in the development of state legislation affecting the use of marihuana, and providing facts and figures for journalistic accounts of the problem. These are two important modes of action available to all entrepreneurs seek-

9. U.S. Treasury Department, *Traffic in Opium and Other Dangerous Drugs for the Year ended December 31, 1931* (Washington: Government Printing Office, 1932), p. 51.

ing the adoption of rules: they can enlist the support of other interested organizations and develop, through the use of the press and other communications media, a favorable public attitude toward the proposed rule. If the efforts are successful, the public becomes aware of a definite problem and the appropriate organizations act in concert to produce the desired rule.

The Federal Bureau of Narcotics cooperated actively with the National Conference of Commissioners on Uniform State Laws in developing uniform laws on narcotics, stressing among other matters the need to control marihuana use.[10] In 1932, the Conference approved a draft law. The Bureau commented:

> The present constitutional limitations would seem to require control measures directed against the intrastate traffic in Indian hemp to be adopted by the several State governments rather than by the Federal Government, and the policy has been to urge the State authorities generally to provide the necessary legislation, with supporting enforcement activity, to prohibit the traffic except for bona fide medical purposes. The proposed uniform State narcotic law . . . with optional text applying to the restriction of traffic in Indian hemp, has been recommended as an adequate law to accomplish the desired purposes.[11]

In its report for the year 1936, the Bureau urged its partners in this cooperative effort to exert themselves more strongly and hinted that Federal intervention might perhaps be necessary:

> In the absence of additional Federal legislation the Bureau of Narcotics can therefore carry on no war of its own against this traffic . . . the drug has come into wide and increasing abuse

10. *Ibid.*, pp. 16–17.
11. Bureau of Narcotics, U.S. Treasury Department, *Traffic in Opium and Other Dangerous Drugs for the Year ended December 31, 1932* (Washington: Government Printing Office, 1933), p. 13.

in many states, and the Bureau of Narcotics has therefore been endeavoring to impress upon the various States the urgent need for vigorous enforcement of local cannabis [marihuana] laws.[12]

The second prong of the Bureau's attack on the marihuana problem consisted of an effort to arouse the public to the danger confronting it by means of "an educational campaign describing the drug, its identification, and evil effects." [13] Apparently hoping that public interest might spur the States and cities to greater efforts, the Bureau said:

In the absence of Federal legislation on the subject, the States and cities should rightfully assume the responsibility of providing vigorous measures for the extinction of this lethal weed, and it is therefore hoped that all public-spirited citizens will earnestly enlist in the movement urged by the Treasury Department to adjure intensified enforcement of marihuana laws.[14]

The Bureau did not confine itself to exhortation in departmental reports. Its methods in pursuing desired legislation are described in a passage dealing with the campaign for a uniform state narcotic law:

Articles were prepared in the Federal Bureau of Narcotics, at the request of a number of organizations dealing with this general subject [uniform state laws] for publication by such organizations in magazines and newspapers. An intelligent and sympathetic public interest, helpful to the administration of the narcotic laws, has been aroused and maintained.[15]

12. Bureau of Narcotics, U.S. Treasury Department, *Traffic in Opium and Other Dangerous Drugs for the Year ended December 31, 1936* (Washington: Government Printing Office, 1937), p. 59.
13. *Ibid.*
14. Bureau of Narcotics, U.S. Treasury Department, *Traffic in Opium and Other Dangerous Drugs for the Year ended December 31, 1935* (Washington: Government Printing Office, 1936), p. 30.
15. Bureau of Narcotics, U.S. Treasury Department, *Traffic in Opium and Other Dangerous Drugs for the Year ended December 31, 1933* (Washington: Government Printing Office, 1934), p. 61.

As the campaign for Federal legislation against marihuana drew to a successful close, the Bureau's efforts to communicate its sense of the urgency of the problem to the public bore plentiful fruit. The number of articles about marihuana which appeared in popular magazines indicated by the number indexed in the *Reader's Guide*, reached a record high. Seventeen articles appeared in a two-year period, many more than in any similar period before or after.

Articles on Marihuana Indexed in
The Reader's Guide to Periodical Literature

Time Period	Number of Articles
January, 1925–December, 1928	0
January, 1929–June, 1932	0
July, 1932–June, 1935	0
July, 1935–June, 1937	4
July, 1937–June, 1939	17
July, 1939–June, 1941	4
July, 1941–June, 1943	1
July, 1943–April, 1945	4
May, 1945–April, 1947	6
May, 1947–April, 1949	0
May, 1949–March, 1951	1

Of the seventeen, ten either explicitly acknowledged the help of the Bureau in furnishing facts and figures or gave implicit evidence of having received help by using facts and figures that had appeared earlier, either in Bureau publications or in testimony before the Congress on the Marihuana Tax Act. (We will consider the Congressional hearings on the bill in a moment.)

One clear indication of Bureau influence in the preparation of journalistic articles can be found in the recurrence of certain atrocity stories first reported by the Bureau. For instance, in an article published in the *American Magazine*, the

141

Commissioner of Narcotics himself related the following incident:

An entire family was murdered by a youthful [marihuana] addict in Florida. When officers arrived at the home they found the youth staggering about in a human slaughterhouse. With an ax he had killed his father, mother, two brothers, and a sister. He seemed to be in a daze. . . . He had no recollection of having committed the multiple crime. The officers knew him ordinarily as a sane, rather quiet young man; now he was pitifully crazed. They sought the reason. The boy said he had been in the habit of smoking something which youthful friends called "muggles," a childish name for marihuana.[16]

Five of the seventeen articles printed during the period repeated this story, and thus showed the influence of the Bureau.

The articles designed to arouse the public to the dangers of marihuana identified use of the drug as a violation of the value of self-control and the prohibition on search for "illicit pleasure," thus legitimizing the drive against marihuana in the eyes of the public. These, of course, were the same values that had been appealed to in the course of the quest for legislation prohibiting use of alcohol and opiates for illicit purposes.

The Federal Bureau of Narcotics, then, provided most of the enterprise which produced public awareness of the problem and coordinated action by other enforcement organizations. Armed with the results of their enterprise, representatives of the Treasury Department went to Congress with a draft of the Marihuana Tax Act and requested its passage. The hearings of the House Committee on Ways and Means, which considered the bill for five days during April and May of 1937, furnish a clear case of the operation of enterprise and of the way it must accommodate other interests.

The Assistant General Counsel of the Treasury Depart-

16. H. J. Anslinger, with Courtney Ryley Cooper, "Marihuana: Assassin of Youth," *American Magazine*, CXXIV (July, 1937), 19, 150.

ment introduced the bill to the Congressmen with these words: "The leading newspapers of the United States have recognized the seriousness of this problem and many of them have advocated Federal legislation to control the traffic in marihuana." [17] After explaining the constitutional basis of the bill —like the Harrison Act, it was framed as a revenue measure —he reassured them about its possible effects on legitimate businesses:

The form of the bill is such, however, as not to interfere materially with any industrial, medical, or scientific uses which the plant may have. Since hemp fiber and articles manufactured therefrom [twine and light cordage] are obtained from the harmless mature stalk of the plant, all such products have been completely eliminated from the purview of the bill by defining the term "marihuana" in the bill so as to exclude from its provisions the mature stalk and its compounds or manufacturers. There are also some dealings in marihuana seeds for planting purposes and for use in the manufacture of oil which is ultimately employed by the paint and varnish industry. As the seeds, unlike the mature stalk, contain the drug, the same complete exemption could not be applied in this instance.[18]

He further assured them that the medical profession rarely used the drug, so that its prohibition would work no hardship on them or on the pharmaceutical industry.

The committee members were ready to do what was necessary and, in fact, queried the Commissioner of Narcotics as to why this legislation had been proposed only now. He explained:

Ten years ago we only heard about it throughout the Southwest. It is only in the last few years that it has become a national menace. . . . We have been urging uniform State legislation on

17. *Taxation of Marihuana* (Hearings before the Committee on Ways and Means of the House of Representatives, 75th Congress, 1st Session, on H.R. 6385, April 27–30 and May 4, 1937), p. 7.

18. *Ibid.*, p. 8.

the several States, and it was only last month that the last State legislature adopted such legislation.[19]

The commissioner reported that many crimes were committed under the influence of marihuana, and gave examples, including the story of the Florida mass-murderer. He pointed out that the present low prices of the drug made it doubly dangerous, because it was available to anyone who had a dime to spare.

Manufacturers of hempseed oil voiced certain objections to the language of the bill, which was quickly changed to meet their specifications. But a more serious objection came from the birdseed industry, which at that time used some four million pounds of hempseed a year. Its representative apologized to the Congressmen for appearing at the last minute, stating that he and his colleagues had not realized until just then that the marihuana plant referred to in the bill was the same plant from which they got an important ingredient of their product. Government witnesses had insisted that the seeds of the plant required prohibition, as well as the flowering tops smokers usually used, because they contained a small amount of the active principle of the drug and might possibly be used for smoking. The birdseed manufacturers contended that inclusion of seed under the provisions of the bill would damage their business.

To justify his request for exemption, the manufacturers' representative pointed to the beneficial effect of hempseed on pigeons:

[It] is a necessary ingredient in pigeon feed because it contains an oil substance that is a valuable ingredient of pigeon feed, and we have not been able to find any seed that will take its place. If you substitute anything for the hemp, it has a tendency to change the character of the squabs produced.[20]

19. *Ibid.*, p. 20.
20. *Ibid.*, pp. 73–74.

Congressman Robert L. Doughton of North Carolina inquired: "Does that seed have the same effect on pigeons as the drug has on human beings?" The manufacturers' representative said: "I have never noticed it. It has a tendency to bring back the feathers and improve the birds." [21]

Faced with serious opposition, the Government modified its stern insistence on the seed provision, noting that sterilization of the seeds might render them harmless: "It seems to us that the burden of proof is on the Government there, when we might injure a legitimate industry." [22]

Once these difficulties had been ironed out, the bill had easy sailing. Marihuana smokers, powerless, unorganized, and lacking publicly legitimate grounds for attack, sent no representatives to the hearings and their point of view found no place in the record. Unopposed, the bill passed both the House and Senate the following July. The enterprise of the Bureau had produced a new rule, whose subsequent enforcement would help create a new class of outsiders—marihuana users.

I have given an extended illustration from the field of Federal legislation. But the basic parameters of this case should be equally applicable not only to legislation in general, but to the development of rules of a more informal kind. Wherever rules are created and applied, we should be alive to the possible presence of an enterprising individual or group. Their activities can properly be called *moral enterprise*, for what they are enterprising about is the creation of a new fragment of the moral constitution of society, its code of right and wrong.

Wherever rules are created and applied we should expect to find people attempting to enlist the support of coordinate groups and using the available media of communication to

21. *Ibid.*
22. *Ibid.*, p. 85.

develop a favorable climate of opinion. Where they do not develop such support, we may expect to find their enterprise unsuccessful.[23]

And, wherever rules are created and applied, we expect that the processes of enforcement will be shaped by the complexity of the organization, resting on a basis of shared understandings in simpler groups and resulting from political maneuvering and bargaining in complex structures.

23. Gouldner has described a relevant case in industry, where a new manager's attempt to enforce rules that had not been enforced for a long time (and thus, in effect, create new rules) had as its immediate consequence a disruptive wildcat strike; he had not built support through the manipulation of other groups in the factory and the development of a favorable climate of opinion. See Alvin W. Gouldner, *Wildcat Strike* (Yellow Springs, Ohio: Antioch Press, 1954).

8 Moral Entrepreneurs

RULES are the products of someone's initiative and we can think of the people who exhibit such enterprise as *moral entrepreneurs*. Two related species—rule creators and rule enforcers—will occupy our attention.

Rule Creators

The prototype of the rule creator, but not the only variety as we shall see, is the crusading reformer. He is interested in the content of rules. The existing rules do not satisfy him because there is some evil which profoundly disturbs him. He feels that nothing can be right in the world until rules are made to correct it. He operates with an absolute ethic; what he sees is truly and totally evil with no qualification. Any means is justified to do away with it. The crusader is fervent and righteous, often self-righteous.

It is appropriate to think of reformers as crusaders because they typically believe that their mission is a holy one. The prohibitionist serves as an excellent example, as does the person who wants to suppress vice and sexual delinquency or the person who wants to do away with gambling.

These examples suggest that the moral crusader is a meddling busybody, interested in forcing his own morals on others. But this is a one-sided view. Many moral crusades have strong humanitarian overtones. The crusader is not only interested in seeing to it that other people do what he thinks right. He believes that if they do what is right it will be good for them. Or he may feel that his reform will prevent certain kinds of exploitation of one person by another. Prohibitionists felt that they were not simply forcing their morals on others, but attempting to provide the conditions for a better way of life for people prevented by drink from realizing a truly good life. Abolitionists were not simply trying to prevent slave owners from doing the wrong thing; they were trying to help slaves to achieve a better life. Because of the importance of the humanitarian motive, moral crusaders (despite their relatively single-minded devotion to their particular cause) often lend their support to other humanitarian crusades. Joseph Gusfield has pointed out that:

The American temperance movement during the 19th century was a part of a general effort toward the improvement of the worth of the human being through improved morality as well as economic conditions. The mixture of the religious, the equalitarian, and the humanitarian was an outstanding facet of the moral

148

reformism of many movements. Temperance supporters formed a large segment of movements such as sabbatarianism, abolition, woman's rights, agrarianism, and humanitarian attempts to improve the lot of the poor. . . .

In its auxiliary interests the WCTU revealed a great concern for the improvement of the welfare of the lower classes. It was active in campaigns to secure penal reform, to shorten working hours and raise wages for workers, and to abolish child labor and in a number of other humanitarian and equalitarian activities. In the 1880's the WCTU worked to bring about legislation for the protection of working girls against the exploitation by men.[1]

As Gusfield says,[2] "Moral reformism of this type suggests the approach of a dominant class toward those less favorably situated in the economic and social structure." Moral crusaders typically want to help those beneath them to achieve a better status. That those beneath them do not always like the means proposed for their salvation is another matter. But this fact—that moral crusades are typically dominated by those in the upper levels of the social structure—means that they add to the power they derive from the legitimacy of their moral position, the power they derive from their superior position in society.

Naturally, many moral crusades draw support from people whose motives are less pure than those of the crusader. Thus, some industrialists supported Prohibition because they felt it would provide them with a more manageable labor force.[3] Similarly, it is sometimes rumored that Nevada gambling interests support the opposition to attempts to legalize gambling in California because it would cut so heavily into their business,

1. Joseph R. Gusfield, "Social Structure and Moral Reform: A Study of the Woman's Christian Temperance Union," *American Journal of Sociology*, LXI (November, 1955), 223.

2. *Ibid.*

3. See Raymond G. McCarthy, editor, *Drinking and Intoxication* (New Haven and New York: Yale Center of Alcohol Studies and The Free Press of Glencoe, 1959), pp. 395–396.

which depends in substantial measure on the population of Southern California.[4]

The moral crusader, however, is more concerned with ends than with means. When it comes to drawing up specific rules (typically in the form of legislation to be proposed to a state legislature or the Federal Congress), he frequently relies on the advice of experts. Lawyers, expert in the drawing of acceptable legislation, often play this role. Government bureaus in whose jurisdiction the problem falls may also have the necessary expertise, as did the Federal Bureau of Narcotics in the case of the marihuana problem.

As psychiatric ideology, however, becomes increasingly acceptable, a new expert has appeared—the psychiatrist. Sutherland, in his discussion of the natural history of sexual psychopath laws, pointed to the psychiatrist's influence.[5] He suggests the following as the conditions under which the sexual psychopath law, which provides that a person "who is diagnosed as a sexual psychopath may be confined for an indefinite period in a state hospital for the insane," [6] will be passed.

First, these laws are customarily enacted after a state of fear has been aroused in a community by a few serious sex crimes committed in quick succession. This is illustrated in Indiana, where a law was passed following three or four sexual attacks in Indianapolis, with murder in two. Heads of families bought guns and watch dogs, and the supply of locks and chains in the hardware stores of the city was completely exhausted. . . .

A second element in the process of developing sexual psychopath laws is the agitated activity of the community in connection with the fear. The attention of the community is focused on sex

4. This is suggested in Oscar Lewis, *Sagebrush Casinos: The Story of Legal Gambling in Nevada* (New York: Doubleday and Co., 1953), pp. 233–234.

5. Edwin H. Sutherland, "The Diffusion of Sexual Psychopath Laws," *American Journal of Sociology*, LVI (September, 1950), 142–148.

6. *Ibid.*, p. 142.

crimes, and people in the most varied situations envisage dangers and see the need of and possibility for their control. . . .

The third phase in the development of these sexual psychopath laws has been the appointment of a committee. The committee gathers the many conflicting recommendations of persons and groups of persons, attempts to determine "facts," studies procedures in other states, and makes recommendations, which generally include bills for the legislature. Although the general fear usually subsides within a few days, a committee has the formal duty of following through until positive action is taken. Terror which does not result in a committee is much less likely to result in a law.[7]

In the case of sexual psychopath laws, there usually is no government agency charged with dealing in a specialized way with sexual deviations. Therefore, when the need for expert advice in drawing up legislation arises, people frequently turn to the professional group most closely associated with such problems:

In some states, at the committee stage of the development of a sexual psychopath law, psychiatrists have played an important part. The psychiatrists, more than any others, have been the interest group back of the laws. A committee of psychiatrists and neurologists in Chicago wrote the bill which became the sexual psychopath law of Illinois; the bill was sponsored by the Chicago Bar Association and by the state's attorney of Cook County and was enacted with little opposition in the next session of the State Legislature. In Minnesota all the members of the governor's committee except one were psychiatrists. In Wisconsin the Milwaukee Neuropsychiatric Society shared in pressing the Milwaukee Crime Commission for the enactment of a law. In Indiana the attorney-general's committee received from the American Psychiatric Association copies of all of the sexual psychopath laws which had been enacted in other states.[8]

7. *Ibid.*, pp. 143–145.
8. *Ibid.*, pp. 145–146.

The influence of psychiatrists in other realms of the criminal law has increased in recent years.

In any case, what is important about this example is not that psychiatrists are becoming increasingly influential, but that the moral crusader, at some point in the development of his crusade, often requires the services of a professional who can draw up the appropriate rules in an appropriate form. The crusader himself is often not concerned with such details. Enough for him that the main point has been won; he leaves its implementation to others.

By leaving the drafting of the specific rule in the hands of others, the crusader opens the door for many unforeseen influences. For those who draft legislation for crusaders have their own interests, which may affect the legislation they prepare. It is likely that the sexual psychopath laws drawn by psychiatrists contain many features never intended by the citizens who spearheaded the drives to "do something about sex crimes," features which do however reflect the professional interests of organized psychiatry.

The Fate of Moral Crusades

A crusade may achieve striking success, as did the Prohibition movement with the passage of the Eighteenth Amendment. It may fail completely, as has the drive to do away with the use of tobacco or the anti-vivisection movement. It may achieve great success, only to find its gains whittled away by shifts in public morality and increasing restrictions imposed on it by judicial interpretations; such has been the case with the crusade against obscene literature.

One major consequence of a successful crusade, of course, is the establishment of a new rule or set of rules, usually with the appropriate enforcement machinery being provided at the same time. I want to consider this consequence at some length later. There is another consequence, however, of the success of a crusade which deserves mention.

When a man has been successful in the enterprise of getting a new rule established—when he has found, so to speak, the Grail—he is out of a job. The crusade which has occupied so much of his time, energy, and passion is over. Such a man is likely, when he first began his crusade, to have been an amateur, a man who engaged in a crusade because of his interest in the issue, in the content of the rule he wanted established. Kenneth Burke once noted that a man's occupation may become his preoccupation. The equation is also good the other way around. A man's preoccupation may become his occupation. What started as an amateur interest in a moral issue may become an almost full-time job; indeed, for many reformers it becomes just this. The success of the crusade, therefore, leaves the crusader without a vocation. Such a man, at loose ends, may generalize his interest and discover something new to view with alarm, a new evil about which something ought to be done. He becomes a professional discoverer of wrongs to be righted, of situations requiring new rules.

When the crusade has produced a large organization devoted to its cause, officials of the organization are even more likely than the individual crusader to look for new causes to espouse. This process occurred dramatically in the field of health problems when the National Foundation for Infantile Paralysis put itself out of business by discovering a vaccine that eliminated epidemic poliomyelitis. Taking the less constraining name of The National Foundation, officials quickly discovered other health problems to which the organization could devote its energies and resources.

The unsuccessful crusade, either the one that finds its

153

mission no longer attracts adherents or the one that achieves its goal only to lose it again, may follow one of two courses. On the one hand, it may simply give up its original mission and concentrate on preserving what remains of the organization that has been built up. Such, according to one study, was the fate of the Townsend Movement.[9] Or the failing movement may adhere rigidly to an increasingly less popular mission, as did the Prohibition Movement. Gusfield has described present-day members of the WCTU as "moralizers-in-retreat." [10] As prevailing opinion in the United States becomes increasingly anti-temperance, these women have not softened their attitude toward drinking. On the contrary, they have become bitter at the formerly "respectable" people who no longer will support a temperance movement. The social class level from which WCTU members are drawn has moved down from the upper-middle class to the lower-middle class. The WCTU now turns to attack the middle class it once drew its support from, seeing this group as the locus of acceptance of moderate drinking. The following quotations from Gusfield's interviews with WCTU leaders give some of the flavor of the "moralizer-in-retreat":

When this union was first organized, we had many of the most influential ladies of the city. But now they have got the idea that we ladies who are against taking a cocktail are a little queer. We have an undertaker's wife and a minister's wife, but the lawyer's and the doctor's wives shun us. They don't want to be thought queer.

We fear moderation more than anything. Drinking has become so much a part of everything—even in our church life and our colleges.

It creeps into the official church boards. They keep it in their

9. Sheldon Messinger, "Organizational Transformation: A Case Study of a Declining Social Movement," *American Sociological Review*, XX (February, 1955), 3–10.

10. Gusfield, *op. cit.*, pp. 227–228.

iceboxes. . . . The minister here thinks that the church has gone far, that they are doing too much to help the temperance cause. He's afraid that he'll stub some influential toes.[11]

Only some crusaders, then, are successful in their mission and create, by creating a new rule, a new group of outsiders. Of the successful, some find they have a taste for crusades and seek new problems to attack. Other crusaders fail in their attempt and either support the organization they have created by dropping their distinctive mission and focusing on the problem of organizational maintenance itself or become outsiders themselves, continuing to espouse and preach a doctrine which sounds increasingly queer as time goes on.

Rule Enforcers

The most obvious consequence of a successful crusade is the creation of a new set of rules. With the creation of a new set of rules we often find that a new set of enforcement agencies and officials is established. Sometimes, of course, existing agencies take over the administration of the new rule, but more frequently a new set of rule enforcers is created. The passage of the Harrison Act presaged the creation of the Federal Narcotics Bureau, just as the passage of the Eighteenth Amendment led to the creation of police agencies charged with enforcing the Prohibition Laws.

With the establishment of organizations of rule enforcers, the crusade becomes institutionalized. What started out as a drive to convince the world of the moral necessity of a new rule finally becomes an organization devoted to the enforcement of the rule. Just as radical political movements turn into organized political parties and lusty evangelical sects become

11. *Ibid.*, pp. 227, 229–230.

staid religious denominations, the final outcome of the moral crusade is a police force. To understand, therefore, how the rules creating a new class of outsiders are applied to particular people we must understand the motives and interests of police, the rule enforcers.

Although some policemen undoubtedly have a kind of crusading interest in stamping out evil, it is probably much more typical for the policeman to have a certain detached and objective view of his job. He is not so much concerned with the content of any particular rule as he is with the fact that it is his job to enforce the rule. When the rules are changed, he punishes what was once acceptable behavior just as he ceases to punish behavior that has been made legitimate by a change in the rules. The enforcer, then, may not be interested in the content of the rule as such, but only in the fact that the existence of the rule provides him with a job, a profession, and a *raison d'être*.

Since the enforcement of certain rules provides justification for his way of life, the enforcer has two interests which condition his enforcement activity: first, he must justify the existence of his position and, second, he must win the respect of those he deals with.

These interests are not peculiar to rule enforcers. Members of all occupations feel the need to justify their work and win the respect of others. Musicians, as we have seen, would like to do this but have difficulty finding ways of successfully impressing their worth on customers. Janitors fail to win their tenants' respect, but develop an ideology which stresses the quasi-professional responsibility they have to keep confidential the intimate knowledge of tenants they acquire in the course of their work.[12] Physicians, lawyers, and other professionals,

12. See Ray Gold, "Janitors Versus Tenants: A Status-Income Dilemma," *American Journal of Sociology*, LVII (March, 1952), 486-493.

more successful in winning the respect of clients, develop elaborate mechanisms for maintaining a properly respectful relationship.

In justifying the existence of his position, the rule enforcer faces a double problem. On the one hand, he must demonstrate to others that the problem still exists: the rules he is supposed to enforce have some point, because infractions occur. On the other hand, he must show that his attempts at enforcement are effective and worthwhile, that the evil he is supposed to deal with is in fact being dealt with adequately. Therefore, enforcement organizations, particularly when they are seeking funds, typically oscillate between two kinds of claims. First, they say that by reason of their efforts the problem they deal with is approaching solution. But, in the same breath, they say the problem is perhaps worse than ever (though through no fault of their own) and requires renewed and increased effort to keep it under control. Enforcement officials can be more vehement than anyone else in their insistence that the problem they are supposed to deal with is still with us, in fact is more with us than ever before. In making these claims, enforcement officials provide good reason for continuing the existence of the position they occupy.

We may also note that enforcement officials and agencies are inclined to take a pessimistic view of human nature. If they do not actually believe in original sin, they at least like to dwell on the difficulties in getting people to abide by rules, on the characteristics of human nature that lead people toward evil. They are skeptical of attempts to reform rule-breakers.

The skeptical and pessimistic outlook of the rule enforcer, of course, is reinforced by his daily experience. He sees, as he goes about his work, the evidence that the problem is still with us. He sees the people who continually repeat offenses, thus definitely branding themselves in his eyes as outsiders. Yet it is not too great a stretch of the imagination to suppose that one of the underlying reasons for the enforcer's pessimism about human nature and the possibilities of reform is that fact that if human nature were perfectible and people could be permanently reformed, his job would come to an end.

In the same way, a rule enforcer is likely to believe that it is necessary for the people he deals with to respect him. If they do not, it will be very difficult to do his job; his feeling of security in his work will be lost. Therefore, a good deal of enforcement activity is devoted not to the actual enforcement of rules, but to coercing respect from the people the enforcer deals with. This means that one may be labeled as deviant not because he has actually broken a rule, but because he has shown disrespect to the enforcer of the rule.

Westley's study of policemen in a small industrial city furnishes a good example of this phenomenon. In his interview, he asked policemen, "When do you think a policeman is justified in roughing a man up?" He found that "at least 37% of the men believed that it was legitimate to use violence to coerce respect." [13] He gives some illuminating quotations from his interviews:

Well, there are cases. For example, when you stop a fellow for a routine questioning, say a wise guy, and he starts talking back to you and telling you you are no good and that sort of thing. You know you can take a man in on a disorderly conduct charge, but you can practically never make it stick. So what you do in a case like that is to egg the guy on until he makes a remark where you can justifiably slap him and, then, if he fights back, you can call it resisting arrest.

Well, a prisoner deserves to be hit when he goes to the point where he tries to put you below him.

13. William A. Westley, "Violence and the Police," *American Journal of Sociology*, LIX (July, 1953), 39.

You've gotta get rough when a man's language becomes very bad, when he is trying to make a fool of you in front of everybody else. I think most policemen try to treat people in a nice way, but usually you have to talk pretty rough. That's the only way to set a man down, to make him show a little respect.[14]

What Westley describes is the use of an illegal means of coercing respect from others. Clearly, when a rule enforcer has the option of enforcing a rule or not, the difference in what he does may be caused by the attitude of the offender toward him. If the offender is properly respectful, the enforcer may smooth the situation over. If the offender is disrespectful, then sanctions may be visited on him. Westley has shown that this differential tends to operate in the case of traffic offenses, where the policeman's discretion is perhaps at a maximum.[15] But it probably operates in other areas as well.

Ordinarily, the rule enforcer has a great deal of discretion in many areas, if only because his resources are not sufficient to cope with the volume of rule-breaking he is supposed to deal with. This means that he cannot tackle everything at once and to this extent must temporize with evil. He cannot do the whole job and knows it. He takes his time, on the assumption that the problems he deals with will be around for a long while. He establishes priorities, dealing with things in their turn, handling the most pressing problems immediately and leaving others for later. His attitude toward his work, in short, is professional. He lacks the naïve moral fervor characteristic of the rule creator.

If the enforcer is not going to tackle every case he knows of at once, he must have a basis for deciding when to enforce the rule, which persons committing which acts to label as

14. *Ibid.*
15. See William A. Westley, "The Police: A Sociological Study of Law, Custom, and Morality" (unpublished Ph.D. dissertation, University of Chicago, Department of Sociology, 1951).

deviant. One criterion for selecting people is the "fix." Some people have sufficient political influence or know-how to be able to ward off attempts at enforcement, if not at the time of apprehension then at a later stage in the process. Very often, this function is professionalized; someone performs the job on a full-time basis, available to anyone who wants to hire him. A professional thief described fixers this way:

> There is in every large city a regular fixer for professional thieves. He has no agents and does not solicit and seldom takes any case except that of a professional thief, just as they seldom go to anyone except him. This centralized and monopolistic system of fixing for professional thieves is found in practically all of the large cities and many of the small ones.[16]

Since it is mainly professional thieves who know about the fixer and his operations, the consequence of this criterion for selecting people to apply the rules to is that amateurs tend to be caught, convicted, and labeled deviant much more frequently than professionals. As the professional thief notes:

> You can tell by the way the case is handled in court when the fix is in. When the copper is not very certain he has the right man, or the testimony of the copper and the complainant does not agree, or the prosecutor goes easy on the defendant, or the judge is arrogant in his decisions, you can always be sure that someone has got the work in. This does not happen in many cases of theft, for there is one case of a professional to twenty-five or thirty amateurs who know nothing about the fix. These amateurs get the hard end of the deal every time. The coppers bawl out about the thieves, no one holds up his testimony, the judge delivers an oration, and all of them get credit for stopping a crime wave. When the professional hears the case immediately preceding his own, he will think, "He should have got ninety years. It's the damn amateurs who cause all the heat in the stores." Or else he thinks, "Isn't it a damn shame for that copper to send that kid

16. Edwin H. Sutherland (editor), *The Professional Thief* (Chicago: University of Chicago Press, 1937), pp. 87–88.

away for a pair of hose, and in a few minutes he will agree to a small fine for me for stealing a fur coat?" But if the coppers did not send the amateurs away to strengthen their records of convictions, they could not sandwich in the professionals whom they turn loose.[17]

Enforcers of rules, since they have no stake in the content of particular rules themselves, often develop their own private evaluation of the importance of various kinds of rules and infractions of them. This set of priorities may differ considerably from those held by the general public. For instance, drug users typically believe (and a few policemen have personally confirmed it to me) that police do not consider the use of marihuana to be as important a problem or as dangerous a practice as the use of opiate drugs. Police base this conclusion on the fact that, in their experience, opiate users commit other crimes (such as theft or prostitution) in order to get drugs, while marihuana users do not.

Enforcers, then, responding to the pressures of their own work situation, enforce rules and create outsiders in a selective way. Whether a person who commits a deviant act is in fact labeled a deviant depends on many things extraneous to his actual behavior: whether the enforcement official feels that at this time he must make some show of doing his job in order to justify his position, whether the misbehaver shows proper deference to the enforcer, whether the "fix" has been put in, and where the kind of act he has committed stands on the enforcer's list of priorities.

The professional enforcer's lack of fervor and routine approach to dealing with evil may get him into trouble with the rule creator. The rule creator, as we have said, is concerned with the content of the rules that interest him. He sees them as the means by which evil can be stamped out. He does not

17. *Ibid.*, pp. 91–92.

understand the enforcer's long-range approach to the same problems and cannot see why all the evil that is apparent cannot be stamped out at once.

When the person interested in the content of a rule realizes or has called to his attention the fact that enforcers are dealing selectively with the evil that concerns him, his righteous wrath may be aroused. The professional is denounced for viewing the evil too lightly, for failing to do his duty. The moral entrepreneur, at whose instance the rule was made, arises again to say that the outcome of the last crusade has not been satisfactory or that the gains once made have been whittled away and lost.

Deviance and Enterprise: A Summary

Deviance—in the sense I have been using it, of publicly labeled wrongdoing—is always the result of enterprise. Before any act can be viewed as deviant, and before any class of people can be labeled and treated as outsiders for committing the act, someone must have made the rule which defines the act as deviant. Rules are not made automatically. Even though a practice may be harmful in an objective sense to the group in which it occurs, the harm needs to be discovered and pointed out. People must be made to feel that something ought to be done about it. Someone must call the public's attention to these matters, supply the push necessary to get things done, and direct such energies as are aroused in the proper direction to get a rule created. Deviance is the product of enterprise in the largest sense; without the enterprise required to get rules made, the deviance which consists of breaking the rule could not exist.

Deviance is the product of enterprise in the smaller and

more particular sense as well. Once a rule has come into existence, it must be applied to particular people before the abstract class of outsiders created by the rule can be peopled. Offenders must be discovered, identified, apprehended and convicted (or noted as "different" and stigmatized for their nonconformity, as in the case of legal deviant groups such as dance musicians). This job ordinarily falls to the lot of professional enforcers who, by enforcing already existing rules, create the particular deviants society views as outsiders.

It is an interesting fact that most scientific research and speculation on deviance concerns itself with the people who break rules rather than with those who make and enforce them. If we are to achieve a full understanding of deviant behavior, we must get these two possible foci of inquiry into balance. We must see deviance, and the outsiders who personify the abstract conception, as a consequence of a process of interaction between people, some of whom in the service of their own interests make and enforce rules which catch others who, in the service of their own interests, have committed acts which are labeled deviant.

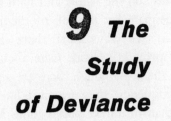

9 The Study of Deviance

PROBLEMS AND SYMPATHIES

THE most persistent difficulty in the scientific study of deviant behavior is a lack of solid data, a paucity of facts and information on which to base our theories. I think it a truism to say that a theory that is not closely tied to a wealth of facts about the subject it proposes to explain is not likely to be very useful. Yet an inspection of the scientific literature on deviant behavior will show that it assays a very high proportion of theory to fact. A critic of studies of juvenile delinquency recently pointed out that the best available source of facts on boys' gangs is still Frederick Thrasher's *The Gang*, first published in 1927.[1]

1. David J. Bordua, "Delinquent Subcultures: Sociological Interpretations of Gang Delinquency," *The Annals of the American Academy of Political and Social Science*, 338 (November, 1961), 119–136.

This is not to say that there are no studies of deviant behavior. There are, but they are, on the whole and with a few outstanding exceptions, inadequate for the job of theorizing we have to do, inadequate in two ways. First, there simply are not enough studies that provide us with facts about the lives of deviants as they live them. Although there are a great many studies of juvenile delinquency, they are more likely to be based on court records than on direct observation. Many studies correlate the incidence of delinquency with such factors as kind of neighborhood, kind of family life, or kind of personality. Very few tell us in detail what a juvenile delinquent does in his daily round of activity and what he thinks about himself, society, and his activities. When we theorize about juvenile delinquency, we are therefore in the position of having to infer the way of life of the delinquent boy from fragmentary studies and journalistic accounts [2] instead of being able to base our theories on adequate knowledge of the phenomenon we are trying to explain. It is as though we tried, as anthropologists once had to do, to construct a description of the initiation rites of some remote African tribe from the scattered and incomplete accounts of a few missionaries. (We have less reason than the anthropologists had for relying on fragmentary amateur descriptions. Their subjects of study were thousands of miles away, in inaccessible jungles; ours are closer to home.)

Studies of deviant behavior are inadequate for theorizing in a second and simpler sense. There are not enough of them. Many kinds of deviance have never been scientifically de-

2. Two well-known and influential recent books on juvenile delinquency are based on such fragmentary data. See Albert K. Cohen, *Delinquent Boys: The Culture of the Gang* (New York: The Free Press of Glencoe, 1955); and Richard A. Cloward and Lloyd E. Ohlin, *Delinquency and Opportunity: A Theory of Delinquent Gangs* (New York: The Free Press of Glencoe, 1960).

scribed, or the studies are so few in number as to be a bare beginning. For instance, how many sociological descriptions are there of the way of life of homosexuals of various kinds? I know of only a few,[3] and these simply make clear that there is a vast variety of cultures and social types to be described. To take an even more extreme case, an area of deviance of utmost importance for sociological theorists has hardly been studied at all. This is the area of professional misconduct. It is well known, for instance, that the ethics committees of legal and medical professional associations have plenty of business to occupy them. Yet, for all the wealth of sociological descriptions of professional behavior and culture, we have few if any studies of unethical behavior by professionals.

What are the consequences of this insufficiency of data for the study of deviance? One consequence, as I have indicated, is the construction of faulty or inadequate theories. Just as we need precise anatomical descriptions of animals before we can begin to theorize about and experiment with their physiological and biochemical functioning, just so we need precise and detailed descriptions of social anatomy before we know just what phenomena are present to be theorized about. To recur to the example of homosexuality, our theories are likely to be quite inadequate if we believe that all homosexuals are more or less confirmed members of homosexual subcultures. A recent study reveals an important group of participants in homosexual relations who are not in the least confirmed homosexuals. Reiss has shown that many juvenile delinquents "hustle queers" as a relatively safe way of picking up money. They do not regard

3. Evelyn Hooker, "A Preliminary Analysis of Group Behavior of Homosexuals," *The Journal of Psychology*, 42 (1956), 217–225; Maurice Leznoff and William A. Westley, "The Homosexual Community," *Social Problems*, 4 (April, 1956), 257–263; H. Laurence Ross, "The 'Hustler' in Chicago," *The Journal of Student Research*, 1 (September, 1959); and Albert J. Reiss, Jr., "The Social Integration of Peers and Queers," *Social Problems*, 9 (Fall, 1961), 102–120.

themselves as homosexuals and when they reach an age to participate in more aggressive and profitable kinds of delinquency they drop the practice.[4] How many other varieties of homosexual behavior await discovery and description? And what effect would their discovery and description have on our theories?

We do not, then, have enough studies of deviant behavior. We do not have studies of enough kinds of deviant behavior. Above all, we do not have enough studies in which the person doing the research has achieved close contact with those he studies, so that he can become aware of the complex and manifold character of the deviant activity.

Some of the reasons for this deficiency are technical. It is not easy to study deviants. Because they are regarded as outsiders by the rest of the society and because they themselves tend to regard the rest of the society as outsiders, the student who would discover the facts about deviance has a substantial barrier to climb before he will be allowed to see the things he needs to see. Since deviant activity is activity that is likely to be punished if it comes to light, it tends to be kept hidden and not exhibited or bragged about to outsiders. The student of deviance must convince those he studies that he will not be dangerous to them, that they will not suffer for what they reveal to him. The researcher, therefore, must participate intensively and continuously with the deviants he wants to study so that they will get to know him well enough to be able to make some assessment of whether his activities will adversely affect theirs.

Those who commit deviant acts protect themselves in various ways from prying outsiders. Deviance within organized conventional institutions is often protected by a kind of cover-up. Thus, members of the professions do not ordinarily

4. Reiss, *op. cit.*

speak about cases of unethical practice in public. Professional associations handle such matters privately, punishing culprits in their own way without publicity. Thus, doctors addicted to narcotics are punished relatively lightly when they come to the attention of law enforcement authorities.[5] A doctor found stealing from hospital narcotics supplies is, ordinarily, simply asked to leave the hospital; he is not turned over to the police. To do research in industrial, educational, and other kinds of large organizations ordinarily requires getting the permission of the people who run those organizations. If the managers of the organization are allowed to, they will limit the area of inquiry in such a way as to hide the deviance they want hidden. Melville Dalton, in describing his own approach to the study of industry, says:

In no case did I make a formal approach to the top management of any of the firms to get approval or support for the research. Several times I have seen other researchers do this and have watched higher managers set the scene and limit the inquiry to specific areas—outside management proper—as though the problem existed in a vacuum. The findings in some cases were then regarded as "controlled experiments," which in final form made impressive reading. But the smiles and delighted manipulation of researchers by guarded personnel, the assessments made of researchers and their findings, and the frequently trivial areas to which altered and fearful officers guided the inquiry—all raised questions about who controlled the experiments.[6]

Members of deviant groups which do not have the covert support of organized professions or establishments use other methods of hiding what they are doing from outside view. Since the activities of homosexuals, drug addicts, and criminals take place without benefit of institutionally locked doors or

5. Charles Winick, "Physician Narcotic Addicts," *Social Problems*, 9 (Fall, 1961), 177.
6. Melville Dalton, *Men Who Manage: Fusions of Feeling and Theory in Administration* (New York: John Wiley and Sons, Inc., 1959), p. 275.

guarded gates, they must devise other means to keep them hidden. Typically, they take great pains to conduct their activities in secret, and such public activities as they engage in take place in relatively controlled areas. For example, there may be a tavern that is a hangout for thieves. While many of the thieves of the city will thus be available in one place to a researcher who wants to study them, they may "dummy up" when he enters the tavern, refusing to have anything to do with him or feigning ignorance of the things he is interested in.

These kinds of secrecy create two research problems. On the one hand, one has the problem of finding the people he is interested in. How does one find a physician who is a drug addict? How does one locate homosexuals of various kinds? If I wanted to study the splitting of fees between surgeons and general medical practitioners, how would I go about finding and getting access to the people who participate in such arrangements? Once found, one has the problem of convincing them that they can safely discuss the problem of their deviance with you.

Other problems present themselves to the student of deviance. If he is to get an accurate and complete account of what deviants do, what their patterns of association are, and so on, he must spend at least some time observing them *in their natural habitat* as they go about their ordinary activities. But this means that the student must, for the time being, keep what are for him unusual hours and penetrate what are for him unknown and possibly dangerous areas of the society. He may find himself staying up nights and sleeping days, because that is what the people he studies do, and this may be difficult because of his commitments to family and work. Furthermore, the process of gaining the confidence of those one studies may be very time consuming so that months may have to be spent in relatively fruitless attempts to gain access. This means that the research takes longer than comparable kinds of research in respectable institutions.

These are technical problems and ways can be found to deal with them. It is more difficult to deal with the moral problems involved in studying deviance.

This is part of the general problem of what viewpoint one ought to take toward his subject of study, of how one shall evaluate things conventionally regarded as evil, of where one's sympathies lie. These problems arise, of course, in studying any social phenomenon. They may be aggravated when we study deviance because the practices and people we study are conventionally condemned.[7]

7. Ned Polsky suggests, in a private communication, that one of the moral problems revolves around the scientist's involvement in illegal activity. Although I have not dealt with this point, I fully agree with his thoughts on the subject, which I reproduce here with his permission:

"If one is effectively to study law-breaking deviants as they engage in their deviance in its natural setting, i.e., outside of jail, he must make the moral decision that in some ways he will break the law himself. He need not be a 'participant observer' and commit the deviant acts under study, yet he has to witness such acts or be taken into confidence about them *and* not blow the whistle. That is, the investigator has to decide that when necessary he will 'obstruct justice' or be an 'accessory' before or after the fact, in the full legal sense of those terms. He will not be enabled to discern some vital aspects of criminally deviant behavior and the structure of law-breaking subcultures unless he makes such a moral decision, makes the deviants believe him, and moreover convinces them of his ability to act in accord with his decision. The last-mentioned point can perhaps be neglected with juvenile delinquents, for they know that a professional studying them is almost always exempt from police pressure to inform; but adult criminals have no such assurance, and hence are concerned not merely with the investigator's intentions but with his sheer ability to remain a 'stand-up guy' under police questioning.

"Social scientists have rarely met these requirements. This is why, despite the fact that in America only about six of every hundred major crimes known to the police result in jail sentences, so much of our alleged sociological knowledge of criminality is based on study of people in jails. The sociologist, unable or unwilling to have himself defined by criminals in a way that would permit him to observe them as they ordinarily go about work and play, typically gathers his data from deviants who are jailed or otherwise enmeshed with the law—a skewed sample who over-represent the nonprofessionals and bunglers, who are seen in artificial settings, and who are not systematically studied as they normally function

In describing social organization and social process—in particular, in describing the organizations and processes involved in deviance—what viewpoint shall we take? Since there are generally several categories of participants in any social organization or process, we must choose between taking the viewpoint of one or another of these groups or the viewpoint of an outside observer. Herbert Blumer has argued that people act by making interpretations of the situation they find themselves in and then adjusting their behavior in such a way as to deal with the situation. Therefore, he continues, we must take the viewpoint of the person or group (the "acting unit") whose behavior we are interested in, and:

. . . catch the process of interpretation through which they construct their actions. . . . To catch the process, the student must take the role of the acting unit whose behavior he is studying. Since the interpretation is being made by the acting unit in terms of objects designated and appraised, meanings acquired, and decisions made, the process has to be seen from the standpoint of the acting unit. . . . To try to catch the interpretive process by remaining aloof as a so-called "objective" observer and refusing to take the role of the acting unit is to risk the worst kind of subjectivism—the objective observer is likely to fill in the process of interpretation with his own surmises in place of catching the process as it occurs in the experience of the acting unit which uses it.[8]

If we study the processes involved in deviance, then, we must take the viewpoint of at least one of the groups involved, either of those who are treated as deviant or of those who label others as deviant.

---

in their natural settings. Thus the sociologist often knows less about truly contemporary deviant subcultures—particularly those composed of adult professional criminals—than the journalist does."

8. Herbert Blumer, "Society as Symbolic Interaction," in Arnold Rose, editor, *Human Behavior and Social Processes: An Interactionist Approach* (Boston: Houghton Mifflin Company, 1962), p. 188.

It is, of course, possible to see the situation from both sides. But it cannot be done simultaneously. That is, we cannot construct a description of a situation or process that in some way fuses the perceptions and interpretations made by both parties involved in a process of deviance. We cannot describe a "higher reality" that makes sense of both sets of views. We can describe the perspectives of one group and see how they mesh or fail to mesh with the perspectives of the other group: the perspectives of rule-breakers as they meet and conflict with the perspectives of those who enforce the rules, and vice versa. But we cannot understand the situation or process without giving full weight to the differences between the perspectives of the two groups involved.

It is in the nature of the phenomenon of deviance that it will be difficult for anyone to study both sides of the process and accurately capture the perspectives of both classes of participants, rule-breakers and rule enforcers. Not that it is impossible, but practical considerations of gaining access to situations and the confidence of the people involved in any reasonable length of time mean that one will probably study the situation from one side or the other. Whichever class of participants we choose to study and whose viewpoint we therefore choose to take, we will probably be accused of "bias." It will be said that we are not doing justice to the viewpoint of the opposing group. In presenting the rationalizations and justifications a group offers for doing things as it does, we will seem to be accepting its rationalizations and justifications and accusing the other parties to the transaction in the words of their opponents. If we study drug addicts, they will surely tell us and we will be bound to report that they believe the outsiders who judge them are wrong and inspired by low motives. If we point to those aspects of the addict's experiences which seem to him to confirm his beliefs, we will seem to be making an apology for the addict. On the other hand, if we view the phenomenon of addiction from the point of view of enforcement officials, they will tell us and we will be bound to report that they believe addicts are criminal types, have disturbed personalities, have no morals, and cannot be trusted. We will be able to point to those aspects of the enforcer's experiences which justify that view. In so doing, we will seem to be agreeing with his view. In either case, we shall be accused of presenting a one-sided and distorted view.

But this is not really the case. What we are presenting is not a distorted view of "reality," but the reality which engages the people we have studied, the reality they create by their interpretation of their experience and in terms of which they act. If we fail to present this reality, we will not have achieved full sociological understanding of the phenomenon we seek to explain.

Whose viewpoint shall we present? There are two considerations here, one strategic and the other temperamental or moral. The strategic consideration is that the viewpoint of conventional society toward deviance is usually well known. Therefore, we ought to study the views of those who participate in deviant activities, because in this way we will fill out the most obscure part of the picture. This, however, is too simple an answer. I suspect that, in fact, we know little enough about the viewpoints of either of the parties involved in phenomena of deviance. While it is true that we do not know much about how deviants themselves view their situations, it is also true that we are not fully aware of, because we have not studied sufficiently, other viewpoints involved. We do not know what all the interests of rule enforcers are. Nor do we know to what extent ordinary members of conventional society actually share, to some degree, the perspectives of deviant groups. David Matza has recently suggested that the characteristic forms of youthful deviance—delinquency, radical politics, and Bohemianism—are in fact subterranean extentions of perspectives held in less extreme form by conventional members of society. Thus, delinquency is a stripped-down version of teen-age culture; radical politics is an extreme version of the vague liberalism contained in the American penchant for "doing good"; and Bohemianism may simply be an extreme version of frivolous college fraternity life, on the one hand, and of the serious intellectual theme in college life on the other.[9] Strategic considerations, then, provide no answer to which viewpoint we should describe.

But neither do temperamental and moral considerations give us an answer. We can, however, be aware of some of the dangers involved. The main danger lies in the fact that deviance has strong connections with feelings of youthful rebelliousness. It is not a matter people take lightly. They feel either that deviance is quite wrong and must be done away with or, on the contrary, that it is a thing to be encouraged—an important corrective to the conformity produced by modern society. The characters in the sociological drama of deviance, even more than characters in other sociological processes, seem to be either heroes or villains. We expose the depravity of deviants or we expose the depravity of those who enforce rules on them.

Both these positions must be guarded against. It is very like the situation with obscene words. Some people think they ought never to be used. Other people like to write them on sidewalks. In either case, the words are viewed as something special, with *mana* of a special kind. But surely it is better to view them simply as words, words that shock some people and

9. David Matza, "Subterranean Traditions of Youth," *The Annals of the American Academy of Political and Social Science*, 338 (November, 1961), 116–118.

delight others. So it is with deviant behavior. We ought not to view it as something special, as depraved or in some magical way better than other kinds of behavior. We ought to see it simply as a kind of behavior some disapprove of and others value, studying the processes by which either or both perspectives are built up and maintained. Perhaps the best surety against either extreme is close contact with the people we study.

10 Labelling Theory Reconsidered

DEVIANT phenomena have long provided one of the foci of sociological thought. Our theoretical interest in the nature of social order combines with practical interest in actions thought harmful to individuals and society to direct our attention to the broad arena of behavior variously called crime, vice, nonconformity, aberration, eccentricity, or madness. Whether we conceive it as a failure of socialization and sanctioning or simply as wrongdoing and

This paper was first presented at the meetings of the British Sociological Association, April, 1971, in London. A number of friends provided helpful comments on an earlier draft. I especially want to thank Eliot Freidson, Blanche Geer, Irving Louis Horowitz, and John I. Kitsuse.

misbehavior, we want to know why people act in disapproved ways.

In recent years, a naturalistic approach to these phenomena (Matza, 1969) has come to center on the interaction between those alleged to be engaged in wrongdoing and those making the allegations. A number of people—Frank Tannenbaum (1938), Edwin Lemert (1951), John Kitsuse (1962), Kai Erikson (1962) and myself (Becker, 1963), to name a few—contributed to the development of what has rather unfortunately been called "labelling theory." Since the initial statements, many people have criticized, extended, and argued over the original statements; others have contributed important research results.

I would like to look back on these developments and see where we stand (cf. Schur, 1969). What has been accomplished? What criticisms have been made? What changes in our conceptions must we make? Three topics especially deserve discussion: the conception of deviance as collective action; the demystification of deviance; and the moral dilemmas of deviance theory. In each case, I intend the point I make to apply to sociological research and analysis generally, reaffirming the faith that the field of deviance is nothing special, just another kind of human activity to be studied and understood.

I might begin by disposing of some seemingly difficult points rather summarily, in a way which will make clear my dissatisfaction with the expression "labelling theory." I never thought the original statements by myself and others warranted being called theories, at least not theories of the fully articulated kind they are now criticized for *not* being. A number of authors complained that labelling theory neither provides an etiological explanation of deviance (Gibbs, 1966; Bordua, 1967; Akers, 1968) nor tells how the people who commit deviant acts come to do that—and especially why *they* do it while others around them do not. Sometimes critics suggest that a theory was proposed, but that it was wrong. Thus, some thought the theory attempted to explain deviance by the responses others made to it. After one was labelled a deviant, according to this paraphrase, then one began to do deviant things, but not before. You can easily dispose of that theory by referring to facts of everyday experience.

The original proponents of the position, however, did not propose solutions to the etiological question. They had more modest aims. They wanted to enlarge the area taken into consideration in the study of deviant phenomena by including in it activities of others than the allegedly deviant actor. They supposed, of course, that when they did that, and as new sources of variance were included in the calculations, all the questions that students of deviance conventionally looked at would take on a different cast.

Further, the act of labelling, as carried out by moral entrepreneurs, while important, cannot possibly be conceived as the sole explanation of what alleged deviants actually do. It would be foolish to propose that stick-up men stick people up simply because someone has labelled them stick-up men, or that everything a homosexual does results from someone having called him homosexual. Nevertheless, one of the most important contributions of this approach has been to focus attention on the way labelling places the actor in circumstances which make it harder for him to continue the normal routines of everyday life and thus provoke him to "abnormal" actions (as when a prison record makes it harder to earn a living at a conventional occupation and so disposes its possessor to move into an illegal one). The degree to which labelling has such effects is, however, an empirical one, to be settled by research into specific cases rather than by theoretical fiat. (See Becker, 1963, pp. 34–35; Lemert, 1951, pp. 71–76; Ray, 1961; and Lemert, 1972.)

Finally, the theory, when it focuses attention on the undeniable actions of those officially in charge of defining deviance, does not make an empirical characterization of the results of particular social institutions. To suggest that defining someone as deviant may under certain circumstances dispose him to a particular line of action is not the same as saying that mental hospitals always drive people crazy or that jails always turn people into habitual criminals.

Labelling achieved its theoretical importance in quite another way. Classes of acts, and particular examples of them, may or may not be thought deviant by any of the various relevant audiences that view them. The difference in definition, in the label applied to the act, makes a difference in what everyone, audiences and actors alike, does subsequently. What the theory did, as Albert Cohen (1965; 1966; 1968) has pointed out, was to create a four-cell property space by combining two dichotomous variables, the commission or noncommission of a given act and the definition of that act as deviant or not. The theory is not a theory about one of the resulting four cells, but a theory about all four of them and their interrelations. In which of those cells we actually locate deviance proper is less important (merely a matter of definition though, like all such matters, not trivial) than understanding that we lose by looking at any one cell alone without seeing it in connection with the others.

My own original formulation created some confusion by referring to one of those variables as "obedient" (as opposed to "rule-breaking") behavior. The distinction implied the prior existence of a determination that rule-breaking had occurred, though, of course, it was just that that the theory proposed to make problematic. I think it better to describe that dimension as the commission or noncommission of a given act. Ordinarily, of course, we study those acts that others are likely to define as deviant; this maximizes our chances of seeing the complicated drama of accusation and definition that is the center of our field of study. Thus, we may be interested in whether a person smokes marihuana, or engages in homosexual acts in public toilets, in part because these acts are likely to be defined as deviant when discovered. We also, of course, study them as phenomena which are interesting in other ways as well. Thus, by studying marihuana use, we can study the way people learn through social interaction to interpret their own physical experience (Becker, 1953). By studying homosexual encounters in public toilets, we can learn how people coordinate their activities through tacit communication (Humphreys, 1970). We can also ask how the high probability that the act will be defined as deviant affects learning the activity and continuing it. It is useful to have a term which indicates that others are likely to define such activities as deviant without making that a scientific judgment that the act is in fact deviant. I suggest we call such acts "potentially deviant."

Labelling theory, then, is neither a theory, with all the achievements and obligations that go with the title, nor focused so exclusively on the act of labelling as some have thought. It is, rather, a way of looking at a general area of human activity; a perspective whose value will appear, if at all, in increased understanding of things formerly obscure. (I will indulge my dislike of the conventional label for the theory by referring to it from now on as an interactionist theory of deviance.)

Deviance as Collective Action

Sociologists agree that what they study is society, but the consensus persists only if we don't look into the nature of society too closely. I prefer to think of what we study

181

as *collective action*. People act, as Mead (1934) and Blumer (1966; 1969) have made clearest, *together*. They do what they do with an eye on what others have done, are doing, and may do in the future. One tries to fit his own line of action into the actions of others, just as each of them likewise adjusts his own developing actions to what he sees and expects others to do. The result of all this adjusting and fitting in can be called a collective action, especially if it is kept in mind that the term covers more than just a conscious collective agreement to, let's say, go on strike, but also extends to participating in a school class, having a meal together, or crossing the street—each of these seen as something being done by a lot of people together.

I don't mean, in using terms like "adjustment" and "fitting in," to suggest an overly peaceful view of social life, or any necessity for people to succumb to social constraints. I mean only that people ordinarily take into account what is going on around them and what is likely to go on after they decide what they will do. The adjusting may consist of deciding that since the police will probably look *here*, I'll put the bomb *there*, as well as of deciding that since the police are going to look, I guess I won't make any bombs at all or even think about it any more.

Neither do I mean, in the foregoing discussion, to imply that social life consists only of face-to-face encounters between individuals. Individuals may engage in intense and persistent interaction though they never encounter one another face-to-face: the interaction of stamp collectors takes place largely through the mail. Further, the give-and-take of interaction, the fitting in and mutual adjustment of lines of activity, occur as well between groups and organizations. The political processes surrounding the drama of deviance have that character. Economic organizations, professional associations, trade unions, lobbyists, moral entreprenuers, and legislators all interact to establish the conditions under which those who represent the state in enforcing laws, for example, interact with those alleged to have violated them.

If we can view any kind of human activity as collective, we can view deviance so. What results? One result is the general view I want to call "interactionist." In its simplest form, the theory insists that we look at all the people involved in any episode of alleged deviance. When we do, we discover that these activities require the overt or tacit cooperation of many people and groups to occur as they do. When workers collude to restrict industrial production (Roy, 1954), they do so with the help of inspectors, maintenance men, and the man in the tool crib. When members of industrial firms steal, they do so with the active cooperation of others above and below them in the firm's hierarchy (Dalton, 1959). Those observations alone cast doubt on theories that seek the origins of deviant acts in individual psychology, for we would have to posit a miraculous meeting of individual forms of pathology to account for the complicated forms of collective activity we observe. Because it is hard to cooperate with people whose reality-testing equipment is inadequate, people suffering from psychological difficulties don't fit well into criminal conspiracies.

When we see deviance as collective action, we immediately see that people act with an eye to the responses of others involved in that action. They take into account the way their fellows will evaluate what they do, and how that evaluation will affect their prestige and rank: The delinquents studied by Short and Strodtbeck (1965) did some of the things they got into trouble for because they wanted to maintain the positions of esteem they held in their gangs.

When we look at all the people and organizations involved in an episode of potentially deviant behavior, we discover too that the collective activity going on consists of more than acts of alleged wrongdoing. It is an involved drama in which making allegations of wrongdoing is a central feature. Indeed, Erikson (1966) and Douglas (1970), among others, have identified the study of deviance as essentially the study of the construction and reaffirmation of moral meanings in everyday social life. Some of the chief actors do not themselves engage in wrongdoing, but rather appear as enforcers of law or morality, as people who complain that other actors are doing wrong, take them into custody, bring them before legal authorities, or administer punishment themselves. If we look long enough and close enough, we discover that they do this sometimes, but not all the time; to some people but not others; in some places but not others. Those discrepancies cast doubt on simple notions about when something is, after all, wrong. We see that the actors themselves often disagree about what is deviant, and often doubt the deviant character of an act. The courts disagree; the police have reservations even when the law is clear; those engaged in the proscribed activity disagree with official definitions. We see, further, that some acts which, by commonly recognized standards, clearly ought to be defined as deviant are not defined that way by anyone. We see that enforcers of law and morality often temporize, allowing some acts to go undetected or unpunished because it would be too much trouble to pursue the matter, because they have limited resources and can't pursue everyone, because the wrongdoer has sufficient power to protect himself from their incursions, because they have been paid to look the other way.

If a sociologist looks for neat categories of crime and deviance and expects to be able to tell clearly when someone has committed one of these acts, so that he can look for its correlates, he finds all these anomalies troublesome. He may hope that they will be disposed of by improved techniques of data gathering and analysis. The long history of attempts to provide those devices ought to tell us the hope is misplaced: That area of human endeavor will not support a belief in the inevitability of progress.

The trouble is not technical. It is theoretical. We can construct workable definitions either of particular actions people might commit or of particular categories of deviance as the world (especially, but not only, the authorities) defines them. But we cannot make the two coincide completely, because they do not do so empirically. They belong to two distinct, though overlapping, systems of collective action. One consists of the people who cooperate to produce the act in question. The other consists of the people who cooperate in the drama of morality by which "wrongdoing" is discovered and dealt with, whether that procedure is formal and legal or quite informal.

Much of the heated discussion over interactionist theories comes from an equivocation in which the word "deviance" is made to stand for two distinct processes taking place in those two systems (a good example is Alvarez, 1968). On the one hand, some analysts want "deviance" to mean acts which, to any "reasonable" member of a society, or by some agreed-on definition (such as violation of an allegedly existent rule, statistical rarity, or psychological pathology), are wrong. They want to focus on the system of action in which those acts occur. The same analysts also want to apply the word to the people who are apprehended and treated as having committed that act. In this case, they want to focus on the system of action in which those judgments occur. This equivocation on the term causes no inaccuracy if and only if those who commit the act and those apprehended are the same. We know they are not. Therefore, if we take as our unit of study those who committed the

act (assuming we can identify them), we necessarily include some who have not been apprehended and labelled;
if we take as our unit those apprehended and labelled, we
necessarily include some who never committed the act but
were treated as if they had (Kitsuse and Cicourel, 1963).

Neither alternative pleases. What interactionist theorists
have done is to treat the two systems as distinct, noting
whatever overlap and interaction occurs between them but
not assuming their occurrence. Thus, one can study the
genesis of drug use, as Lindesmith (1968) and I did, and deal
with etiological questions, never supposing, however, that
what the people studied do has any necessary connection
with a generalized quality of deviance. Or one can, as many
recent studies have done (e.g., Gusfield, 1963), study the
drama of moral rhetoric and action in which imputations of
deviance are made, accepted, rejected, and fought over. The
chief effect of interactionist theory has been to focus attention on that drama as an object of study, and especially to
focus on some relatively unstudied participants in it—those
sufficiently powerful to make their imputations of deviance
stick: police, courts, physicians, school officials, and parents.

I intended my own original formulations to emphasize
the logical independence of acts and the judgments people
made of them. That formulation, however, contained ambiguities that bordered on self-contradiction, especially in connection with the notion of "secret deviance."[1] Examining
those ambiguities and some possible resolutions of them shows
us that fruitful development of the theory probably lies in
a more detailed analysis than we have yet made of deviance
as collective action.

If we begin by saying that an act is deviant when it is so
defined, what can it mean to call an act an instance of secret

1. Jack Katz and John I. Kitsuse helped me greatly in the reanalysis of
the problem of secret deviance.

deviance? Since no one has defined it as deviant it cannot, by definition, be deviant; but "secret" indicates that *we* know it is deviant, even if no one else does. Lorber partially resolved this paradox (1967) by suggesting that in an important class of cases the actor himself defined what he did as deviant, even though he managed to keep others from finding out about it, either believing that it really was deviant or recognizing that others would believe that.

But what if the actor failed to make that definition? What if, even more telling, there were no acts that scientists would recognize as capable of being so defined? (I have in mind here such offenses as witchcraft [Selby, unpublished]; we cannot imagine a case of a secret witch, since we "know" that no one can actually copulate with the Devil, or summon demons.) In neither case can we count on self-definition to resolve the paradox. But we can extend Lorber's idea by seeing that it implies a procedure which, were it applied by the appropriate people, would lead them to make such a judgment, given the "facts" of the particular case. People who believe in witches have ways of deciding when an act of witchcraft has been committed. We may know enough about the circumstances to know that, if those people use such methods, what they discover will lead them to conclude that witchcraft has occurred. In the case of less imaginary offenses, we may know, for instance, that a person has in his pocket materials which, should the police search him, would make him liable to a charge of possession of drugs.

In other words, secret deviance consists of being vulnerable to the commonly used procedures for discovering deviance of a particular kind, of being in a position where it will be easy to make the definition stick. What makes this distinctively collective is the collectively accepted character of the procedures of discovery and proof.

Even with this addition, however, difficulties remain. In

another important class of cases—the construction of rules *ex post facto*—there can have been no secret deviance because the rule did not exist until after the act in question was alleged to have been committed (Katz, 1972). Case-finding procedures might elicit the facts that someone later uses to prove commission of a deviant act, but the person could not have been deviant, secretly or otherwise, because the rule did not exist. Yet he might well be defined as deviant, perhaps when what he might have done becomes public and someone decides that if there was no rule against it, there ought to be. Was he then secretly deviant before?

The paradox resolves itself when we recognize that, like all other forms of collective activity, the acts and definitions in the drama of deviance take place over time, and differ from one time to the next. Definitions of behavior occur sequentially, and an act may be defined as non-deviant at t_1 and deviant at t_2 without implying that it was both simultaneously. Making use of our previous result, we see that an act might *not* be secretly deviant at t_1 because no procedure then in use would produce evidence of an act which competent judges would take to be deviant. The same act *might* be secretly deviant at t_2 because, a new rule having been made in the interim, a procedure now existed which would allow that determination.

The last formulation reminds us of the important role that power plays in interactionist theories of deviance (Horowitz and Liebowitz, 1968). Under what circumstances do we make and enforce *ex post facto* rules? I think empirical investigation will show that it occurs when one party to a relationship is disproportionately powerful, so that he can enforce his will over others' objections but wishes to maintain an appearance of justice and rationality. This characteristically occurs in the relations of parents and children, and in such similarly paternalistic arrangements as welfare worker and client, or teacher and student.

By viewing deviance as a form of collective activity, to be investigated in all its facets like any other form of collective activity, we see that the object of our study is not an isolated act whose origin we are to discover. Rather, the act alleged to occur, when it has occurred, takes place in a complex network of acts involving others, and takes on some of that complexity because of the way various people and groups define it. The lesson applies to our studies of every other area of social life. Learning it will not free us from error fully, however, for our own theories and methods present persistent sources of trouble.

Demystifying Deviance

Sociologists have made trouble for themselves by their virtually unbreakable habit of making common events and experiences mysterious. I remember—one of my first experiences in graduate school—Ernest Burgess warning our class of novices against being led astray by common sense. At the same time, Everett Hughes enjoined us to pay close attention to what we could see and hear with our own eyes and ears. Some of us thought there might be a contradiction between the two imperatives, but suppressed our worry to save our sanity.

Both injunctions have a substantial kernel of truth. Common sense, in one of its meanings, can delude us. This common sense is the traditional wisdom of the tribe, the melange of "what everybody knows" that children learn as they grow up, the stereotypes of everyday life. It includes social-science generalizations about the nature of social phenomena, correlations between social categories (e.g., between race and crime, or class and intelligence), and the etiology of problematic social conditions like poverty and war. Common-sense generalizations resemble those of social science in formal structure; they differ largely in their immunity to contradictory observations. Social-science generalizations, in principle and often in fact, change when new observations show them incorrect. Common-sense generalizations don't. This kind of common sense, particularly because its errors are not random, favors established institutions.

Another meaning of common sense suggests that the common man, his head unencumbered by fancy theories and abstract professorial notions, can at least see what is right there in front of his nose. Philosophies as disparate as pragmatism and Zen enshrine a respect for the common man's ability to see, with Sancho Panza, that a windmill is really a windmill. To think it a knight on horseback is, however you look at it, a real mistake.

Sociologists often ignore the injunctions of this version of common sense. We may not turn windmills into knights. But we often turn collective activity—people doing things together—into abstract nouns whose connection to people doing things together is tenuous. We then typically lose interest in the more mundane things people are actually doing. We ignore what we see because it is not abstract, and chase after the invisible "forces" and "conditions" we have learned to think sociology is all about.

Novice sociologists frequently have great trouble doing field research because they do not recognize sociology, as they have read it, in the human activity they see all around them. They spend eight hours observing a factory or a school, and return with two pages of notes and the explanation that "nothing much happened." They mean that they observed no instances of anomie or stratification or bureaucracy or any of the other conventional sociological topics. They don't see that we invented those terms to enable us to deal conveniently with a number of instances of people doing things together which we have decided are sufficiently alike in specific ways for us to treat them as the same for analytic purposes. Disdaining common sense, novices ignore what happens all around them. Failing to record the details of everyday life in their notes, they cannot use them to study such abstractions as anomie, or others they might themselves construct. An important methodological problem is to systematize the procedure by which we move from an appreciation of ethnographic detail to concepts useful in addressing problems we have come to our research with or have since become aware of.

Conversely, the people sociologists study often have trouble recognizing themselves and their activities in the sociological reports written about them. We ought to worry about that more than we do. We should not expect laymen to make our analyses for us. But neither should we ignore those matters laymen habitually take into account when we describe, or make assumptions about, how they carry on their activities. Many theories of deviance posit, implicitly or explicitly, that a particular set of attitudes underlies commission of some potentially rule-violating act, even though the theory bases itself on data (such as official records) which cannot speak to this point. Consider the descriptions of the actor's state of mind found in theorizing about anomie, from Durkheim through Merton to Cloward and Ohlin. If the people studied cannot recognize themselves in those descriptions without coaching, we should pay attention.

It is not only the descriptions of their own mental states that actors cannot recognize. They often cannot recognize the acts they are supposed to have engaged in, because the sociologist has not observed those acts closely, or paid any attention to their details when he has. The omission has serious results. It makes it impossible for us to put the real contingencies of action into our theories, to make them take account of the constraints and opportunities actually present. We may find ourselves theorizing about activities which never occur in the way we imagine.

If we look closely at what we observe we will very likely see the matters to which interactionist theory calls attention. We see that people who engage in acts conventionally thought deviant are not motivated by mysterious, unknowable forces. They do what they do for much the same reasons that justify more ordinary activities. We see that social rules, far from being fixed and immutable, are continually constructed anew in every situation, to suit the convenience, will, and power position of various participants. We see that activities thought deviant often require elaborate networks of cooperation such as could hardly be sustained by people suffering from disabling mental difficulties. Interactionist theory may be an almost inevitable consequence of submitting our theories of deviance to the editing of close observation of the things they purport to be about.

Insofar as both common sense and science enjoin us to look at things closely before we start theorizing about them, obedience to the injunction produces a complex theory that takes into account the actions and reactions of everyone involved in episodes of deviance. It leaves for empirical determination (instead of settling by assumption) such matters as whether the alleged acts actually occurred, and whether official reports are accurate and to what degree. In consequence (and this is a source of great difficulty to older styles of deviance research), great doubt arises as to the utility of the various statistical series and official records researchers have been accustomed to use. I will not rehearse the major criticisms of official records, the defenses that have been made of them, and the new uses suggested for them, but simply note that a closer look at people acting together has made us aware that records are also produced by people acting together, and must be understood in that context. (See Cicourel and Kitsuse, 1963; Garfinkel and Bittner, 1967; Cicourel, 1968; Biderman and Reiss, 1967; Douglas, 1967.)

The connection between an interactionist theory of deviance and a reliance on intensive field observation as a major method of data-gathering can hardly be accidental. On the other hand, I think it is not a necessary connection. Interactionist theory grows out of a frame of mind that takes the commonplace seriously and will not settle for mysterious invisible forces as explanatory mechanisms. That frame of mind undoubtedly flourishes when one continually confronts the details of the things he proposes to explain in all their complexity. It is easier to construct mythical wrongdoers, and give them whatever qualities go best with our hypothesized explanations, if we have only such fragments of fact as we might find in an official folder or in the answers to a questionnaire. As Galtung (1965) has suggested in another connection, mythical constructs cannot defend themselves against the onslaught of contrary fact produced by intimate acquaintance.

Some people have noted that too great an emphasis on first-hand observation may cause us unintentionally to limit ourselves to those groups and sites we can easily get access to, thus failing to study the powerful people and groups who can defend themselves against our incursions. In this way, preference for an observational technique could work against the theoretical recommendation to study all parties to the drama of deviance, and undo some of the advantages of an interactionist approach. We can guard against this danger both by varying our methods and by being more ingenious in our use of observational techniques. Mills (1956), among others, demonstrates the variety of methods that can be used to study the powerful, and especially the study of those documents that become public through inadvertence, by virtue of the workings of governmental agencies, or because the powerful sometimes fight among themselves and provide data for us when they do. Similarly, we can make use of techniques of unobtrusive entry and accidental access (Becker and Mack, 1971) to gather direct observational data. (Relevant problems of access and sampling are discussed in several papers in Habenstein, 1970.)

Sociologists have generally been reluctant to take the close look at what sits in front of their noses I have recommended here. That reluctance especially infected deviance studies. Overcoming it has produced the same gain in studies of deviance that similar moves produced in studies of industry, education, and communities. It also increased the moral complexity of our theories and research, and I turn to those problems now.

Moral Problems

Moral problems arise in all sociological research but are especially provocatively posed by interactionist theories of deviance. Moral criticism has come from the political center and beyond; from the political Left, and from left field. Interactionist theories have been accused of giving aid and comfort to the enemy, be the enemy those who would upset the stability of the existing order or the Establishment. They have been accused of openly espousing unconventional norms, of refusing to support anti-Establishment positions, and (the left-field position) of appearing to support anti-Establishment causes while subtly favoring the *status quo*.

Interactionist theories as subversive. Many critics (not necessarily conservative, though some are) believe that interactionist theories of deviance openly or covertly attack conventional morality, willfully refusing to accept its definitions of what is and is not deviant, and calling into question the assumptions on which conventional organizations dealing with deviance operate. Lemert, for instance, says:

On the surface deviance sociology seems to offer a relatively detached or scientific way of studying certain types of social problems. Yet its mood and tone and choice of research subjects disclose a strong fixed critical stance toward the ideology, values and methods of state dominated agencies of social control. In extreme statements deviance is portrayed as little more than the result of arbitrary, fortuitous, or biased decision-making, to be understood as a sociopsychological process by which groups seek to create conditions for perpetuating established values and ways of behaving or enhancing the power of special groups. One impression left is that agencies of social control are described and analyzed to expose their failures in what they try to do and their incidental encroachments on "inalienable rights" and "freedom." Thus seen, deviance sociology is more social criticism than science. It offers little to facilitate and foster the kinds of decisions and controls actually necessary to maintain the unique quality of our society—the freedom to choose. (Lemert, 1972, p. 24)

Such critics think that the principled determination to treat official and conventional viewpoints as things to be studied, instead of accepting them as fact or self-evident truth, is a mischievous assault on the social order (Bordua, 1967).

Consider again the criticism that "labelling theory" irremediably confuses what it proposed to explain with its explanation. If it treats deviance solely as a matter of definition by those who react to it, but simultaneously posits a deviant-something-to-which-they-react, then the deviance must somehow exist prior to the reaction. Some critics do not focus on the real logical difficulties I considered earlier, but rather insist that there must be some quality of an act that can be taken as deviant, independent of anyone's reaction. They usually find that quality in the act's violation of an agreed-on rule (e.g., Gibbs, 1966; Alvarez, 1968). They think theorists who will not admit that some acts are *really* deviant, at least in the sense of rule violation, perverse.

But interactionist theorists, not especially perverse, have emphasized the independence of act and reaction, creating a property space of four cells by combining the commission or noncommission of a potentially deviant act with a deviance-defining reaction or its absence. What seems to have bothered critics in this procedure is that the term "deviance" has then more often been applied to the pair of cells characterized by acts defined as deviant, whether the alleged acts occurred or not. The choice probably reflects analysts' unwillingness to seem to approve the derogatory classification of potentially deviant acts. The unwillingness arises out of their recognition of the intrinsically situational character of rules, which exist only in the perpetually renewed consensus of one situation after another rather than as persisting specific embodiments of basic value (see the concept of "negotiated order" in Strauss *et al.*, 1964).

In any event, had interactionsts typically called deviant the commission of potentially deviant acts, whatever the reaction to them, fewer would have complained. Many of us used the term loosely to cover all three cases in which deviance might be implicated: commission of a potentially deviant act without deviance-defining; deviance-defining without commission; and their co-existence. That sloppiness deserves criticism, but the important point is that no one of these is itself the whole story of deviance. That lies in the interaction among all the parties involved.

To return to the larger point, the real attack on the social order is to insist that all parties involved are fit objects of study. The earlier definition of the field of deviance as the study of people alleged to have violated rules respected that order by exempting the creators and enforcers of those rules from study. To be exempted from study means that one's claims, theories, and statements of fact are not subjected to critical scrutiny (Becker, 1967).

The interactionist reluctance to accept conventional theories has led to a critical attitude toward the assertions of conventional authority and morality, and to a hostility toward interactionist analyses on the part of their spokesmen and defenders. Thus, police officials assert that most policemen are honest except for the few rotten apples found in every barrel. Sociological investigations showing that police misbehavior results from structural imperatives built into the organization of police work provoke "defenses" of the police against social scientists. Similarly, the assertion that mental illness is a matter of social definition (e.g., Scheff, 1966) provokes the reply that people in mental hospitals are really sick (Gove, 1970a, 1970b), an answer which misses the point of the definitional argument but hits at the implied moral one by suggesting that psychiatrists, after all, know what they're doing.

Interactionist theories as establishmentarian. For the reasons just suggested, interactionist theories look (and are) rather Left. Intentionally or otherwise, they are corrosive of conventional modes of thought and established institutions. Nevertheless, the Left has criticized those theories, and in a way that mirrors more middle-of-the-road objections.[2] Just

2. Richard Berk has suggested to me that the chronic difficulty in deciding who is Left or "radical" leads to a situation in which the criticisms I am discussing, while they may come from people who so identify themselves and are so identified by some others, nevertheless do not flow out of a Marxist analysis of society which has perhaps a better claim to the label. He suggests further that such a line of criticism might focus on the degree to which it is possible to establish a continuity between the analysis of society-wide class groupings characteristic of that tradition and the more intensive study of smaller units characteristic of interactionist theories of deviance. I think the continuity exists, but am not in a position to argue the point analytically.

as people who approve existing institutions dislike the way interactionist theories call their assumptions and legitimacy into question, people who think existing institutions rotten complain that interactionist theories fail to say that those institutions are rotten. Both complain of an ambiguous moral stance, locating the trouble in an unfortunate "value-free" ideology which pretends to neutrality while in fact espousing either a "radical" or "merely liberal" ideology, as the case may be (Mankoff, 1970; Liazos, 1972).

The trouble evidently comes from some equivocation over the notion of being value free. I take it that all social scientists agree that, given a question and a method of reaching an answer, any scientist, whatever his political or other values, should arrive at much the same answer, an answer given by the world of recalcitrant fact that is "out there" whatever we think about it. Insofar as a left-wing sociologist proposes to base political action on his own or others' research findings, he had better strive for this and hope it can be done. Otherwise, his actions may fail because of what his values prevented him from seeing.

That simple formulation cannot be objectionable. But all social scientists miss that goal to some degree, and the missing may result in one way or another from the scientist's values. We may miscount black citizens in the census because we do not think it worth the extra trouble it may take, given their life style, to look for them. We may fail to investigate police corruption because we think it unlikely that it exists— or because it would be unseemly to call attention to it if it did. We may suggest that we can understand political protest by examining the personalities of protestors, thereby implying that the institutions they protest against play no part in the development of their acts of dissidence. We may do work which will be helpful to authorities in dealing with troublemakers, as would be the case were we to discover correlates of radicalism that school authorities, employers, and police could use to weed out potential troublemakers.

The moral questions become more pressing as we move from the technical notion of value freedom to the choice of problems, ways of stating problems, and uses to which findings can be put. Some of these troubles follow from sociology's failure to take itself seriously, to follow the injunction that almost every version of our basic theory contains but which is perhaps clearest in interactionist theory (Blumer, 1967): to study all the parties to a situation, and their relationships. Following that injunction automatically leads us to police corruption where it exists and has anything to do with what we are studying. Following it, we would not study political protest as though it involved only the protestors. A value-free sociology which rigorously followed its own precepts would not trouble the Left this way.

The question of the use of the findings cannot be settled so easily, however. Nor can the question that has plagued many professional associations: whether professional sociologists have any right to a special opinion, by virtue of being sociologists, on moral and political questions. We can see that they might, where it is warranted, claim expertise with respect to the consequences of various policies. And we can see that they might be especially concerned about whose interests they were serving. But we find it harder to substantiate the assertion that the sociologist, by virtue of his science, has any special knowledge, or claim on our attention, with respect to moral questions. Why? Because science, we say, is value-free. We then go on to make tenuous distinctions, impossible to maintain in practice, between the sociologist as scientist and the sociologist as citizen. For we all agree that the citizen–sociologist not only may take moral positions, but cannot avoid doing so.

We cannot maintain these distinctions in practice because,

as Edel [3] (1955) has so tellingly argued, ascertaining facts, constructing scientific theories, and arriving at ethical judgments cannot be so neatly separated. While you cannot logically deduce what *ought* to be done from premises about what *is*, responsible ethical judgments depend very much on our assessment of the way the world and its components are constructed, how they work, what they are capable of. Those assessments rest on good scientific work. They color our ethical decisions by making us see the full moral complexity of what we study; the particular way our general ethical commitments are embodied in a given situation; how our contingent ethical commitments to values like justice, health, mercy, or reason intersect, converge, and conflict.

Our work speaks continuously to ethical questions; it is continuously informed and directed by our ethical concerns. We don't want our values to interfere with our assessment of the validity of our propositions about social life, but we cannot help their influencing our choice of propositions to investigate, or the uses to which we put our findings. Nor should we mind that they do. Simultaneously, our ethical judgments cannot help being influenced by the increasing knowledge our scientific work confronts them with. Science and ethics interpenetrate.

Take marihuana use. Our judgment must change when we shift our view of it from a picture of unbridled indulgence in perverse pleasure to one of a merciless psychic compulsion to tranquilize inner conflict, as psychiatric theories and data proposed. Our judgment changes again when we view it as a relatively harmless recreation whose worst consequences, social and individual, seem to arise from how nonusers react to users. (See Kaplan, 1970; Goode, 1970.) Those of us con-

3. Irving Louis Horowitz prompted my belated acquaintance with the work of Abraham Edel.

cerned with maximizing human freedom will now concentrate on the question of the relative harm caused by the indulgence of pleasure as opposed to its repression. We might study the operation of enforcement systems, the development of vested interests among the bureaucrats and entrepreneurs who operate them, the forces that divert them from their intended aims, the irrelevance of their intended aims to the situations and consequences of uses—all this by way of pursuing the value of freedom. We would be prepared to discover that the premises on which our inquiries are based are incorrect (that, for example, enforcement systems do operate efficiently and honestly to deal with serious troubles for individuals and communities), and we would conduct our research so as to make such discovery possible.

Sociologists beginning from other ethical positions might investigate the pressures of peers, the mass media, and other sources of personal influence that lead to drug use and thus to the breakdown of social order via the mechanism of release from moral constraints. They might look into the subtle way those pressures force people to use drugs and thus limit freedom in the general way feared by earlier psychological theories, even though the mechanism involved differed. They too would be prepared to find their premises and hypotheses invalid. Sociologists who failed to look into the matter at all would thereby signify their belief that it was morally proper to ignore it.

Interactionist theories of deviance come under fire when critics find this complex picture of the relations between scientific research and ethical judgment overly subtle and insufficiently forthright. Just as centrist critics complain of interactionist theory's perverse unwillingness to acknowledge that rape, robbery, and murder are *really* deviant, so Left critics argue that it refuses to recognize that class oppression, racial discrimination, and imperialism are *really* deviant, or that poverty and injustice are *really* social problems, however people define them (Mankoff, 1968).[4] Both sides want to see their ethical preconceptions incorporated into scientific work in the form of uninspected factual assertions relying on the implicit use of ethical judgments about which there is a high degree of consensus.

Thus, if I say that rape is *really* deviant or imperialism *really* a social problem, I imply that those phenomena have certain empirical characteristics which, we would all agree, make them reprehensible. We might, by our studies, be able to establish just that; but we are very often asked to accept it by definition. Defining something as deviant or as a social problem makes empirical demonstration unnecessary and protects us from discovering that our preconception is incorrect (when the world isn't as we imagine it). When we protect our ethical judgments from empirical tests by enshrining them in difinitions, we commit the error of sentimentalism.[5]

Scientists often wish to make it appear that some com-

4. The following statement embodies these themes neatly: "But is it not as much a *social fact*, even though few of us pay much attention to it, that the corporate economy kills and maims more, is more violent, than any violence committed by the poor (the usual subjects of studies of violence)? By what reasoning and necessity is the 'violence' of the poor in the ghettoes more worthy of our attention than the military bootcamps which numb recruits from the horrors of killing the 'enemy' ('Oriental human beings,' as we learned during the Calley trial)? But because these acts are not labelled 'Deviant,' because they are covert, institutional, and normal, their 'deviant' qualities are overlooked and they do not become part of the province of the sociology of deviance. Despite their best liberal intentions, these sociologists seem to perpetuate the very notions they think they debunk, and others of which they are unaware." (Liazos, 1972, pp. 110–111)

5. At least one critic (Gouldner, 1968) has misread my criticism of sentimentalism as a fear of emotion. The definition given in the text of "Whose Side Are We On?" (Becker, 1967, p. 245) makes my actual meaning quite clear: "We are sentimental, especially, when our reason is that we would prefer not to know what is going on, if to know would be to violate some sympathy whose existence we may not even be aware of."

plicated combination of sociological theories, scientific evidence, and ethical judgments is really no more than a simple matter of definition. Scientists who have made strong value commitments (of whatever political or moral variety) seem especially likely to want that. Why do people want to disguise their morals as science? Most likely, they realize or intuit the contemporary rhetorical advantage of not having to admit that it is "only a moral judgment" one is making, and pretending instead that it is a scientific finding. All parties to any major social and moral controversy will attempt to gain that advantage and present their moral position as so axiomatic that it can be built into the presuppositions of their theory, research, and political dogma, without question. I suggest to the Left, whose sympathies I share, that we should attack injustice and oppression directly and openly, rather than pretend that the judgment that such things are evil is somehow deducible from sociological first principles, or warranted by empirical findings alone.

Our ethical dispositions and judgments, while they properly play a part in our scientific work, should play a different role in the various activities that constitute a sociologist's work. When we test our hypotheses and propositions against empirical evidence we try to minimize their influence, fearing that wishful thinking will color our conclusions. When we select problems for research, however, we take into account (along with such practical matters as our ability to gain access, and such theoretical concerns as the likelihood of achieving powerful general conclusions) the bearing of our potential findings on ethical problems we care about. We want to find out whether our initial judgments are correct, what possibilities of action are open to us and to other actors in the situation, what good might be accomplished with the knowledge we hope to gather. When we decide what actions to take on the basis of our findings, and when we decide whom to give advice to, our ethical commitments clearly dominate our choices—though we still want to be accurate in our assessment of the consequences of any such act. Finally, we sometimes begin with the actions we want to take and the people we want to help, as a basis for choosing problems and methods.

The criticism from left field. Some critics (e.g., Gouldner, 1968) have argued that interactionist theories of deviance, while appearing anti-Establishment, in fact support the Establishment by attacking lower-level functionaries of oppressive institutions, leaving the higher-ups responsible for the oppression unscathed and, indeed, assisting them by blowing the whistle on their unruly underlings.

In the present state of our knowledge, we can only deal with such questions speculatively. No evidence has been adduced to support the criticism, nor could one readily find evidence to refute it. The criticism speaks to the general moral thrust of interactionist theories, as well as to factual questions of the consequences of research and theorizing, and can be challenged on that ground.

Interactionist theories of deviance, like interactionist theories generally, pay attention to how social actors define each other and their environments. They pay particular attention to differentials in the power to define; in the way one group achieves and uses the power to define how other groups will be regarded, understood, and treated. Elites, ruling classes, bosses, adults, men, Caucasians—superordinate groups generally—maintain their power as much by controlling how people define the world, its components, and its possibilities, as by the use of more primitive forms of control. They may use more primitive means to establish hegemony. But control based on the manipulation of definitions and labels works more smoothly and costs less; superordinates prefer it. The attack on hierarchy begins with an attack on definitions, labels, and conventional conceptions of who's who and what's what.

History has moved us increasingly in the direction of disguised modes of control based on control of the definitions and labels applied to people. We exert control by accusing people of deviant acts of various kinds. In the United States, we indict political dissidents for using illegal drugs. Almost every modern state makes use of psychiatric diagnoses, facilities, and personnel to confine politically troublesome types as varied as Ezra Pound or Z. A. Medvedev (Szasz, 1965). When we study how moral entrepreneurs get rules made and how enforcers apply those rules in particular cases, we study the way superordinates of every description maintain their positions. To put it another way, we study some of the forms of oppression, and the means by which oppression achieves the status of being "normal," "everyday," and legitimate.

Most research on deviance in the interactionist mode has concentrated on the immediate participants in localized dramas of deviance: those who engage in various forms of crime and vice, and those enforcers they meet in their daily rounds. We have tended more to study policemen, mental-hospital attendants, prison guards, psychiatrists, and the like, and less their superiors or their superiors' superiors. (There are exceptions: Messinger's [1969] study of prison administration; Dalton's [1959] study of industrial managers; Skolnick's [1969] application of deviance theory to the politics of protest in the United States.)

But the focus on lower-level authorities not only is neither exclusive nor inevitable; its actual effect is to cast doubt on higher-level authorities who are responsible for the actions of their subordinates. They may explicitly order those actions, order them in Aesopian language so that they can deny having done it if necessary, or simply allow them to occur through incompetence or oversight. If the actions are reprehensible, then higher authorities, one way or another, share in the blame. Even if no general is ever brought to trail for the killings at My Lai, those events shook such faith as people had in the moral correctness of the military action in Vietnam and of those at the highest levels responsible for it. Similarly, when we understand how school psychiatrists operate as agents of school officials rather than of their patients (Szasz, 1967), we lose some of whatever faith we had in the institutions of conventional psychiatry. The rapidity with which official spokesmen at the highest levels move to counter analyses of even the lowest-level corruption, incompetence, or injustice should let us see at least as clearly as they do the degree to which those analyses attack institutions as well as their agents, and superiors as well as their subordinates. Such research has special moral sting to it when it allows us to inspect the practice of an institution in the light of its own professed aims and its own preferred descriptions of what it is about. Because of that, our work invariably has a critical thrust when it produces anything that can be construed as an evaluation of the operations of a society or any of its parts.

Conclusion

The interactionist approach to deviance has served not only to clarify the phenomena that have conventionally been studied under that rubric but also to complicate our moral view of them. The interactionist approach begins that double task of clarification and complication by making sociologists aware that a wider range of people and events needs to be included in our study of deviant phenomena, by sensitizing us to the importance of a wider range of fact. We study all the participants in these moral dramas, accusers as well as accused, offering a conventional exemption from our professional inquiries to no one, no matter how respectable or highly placed. We look carefully at the actual activities in question, attempting to understand the contingencies of action for everyone concerned. We accept no invocation of mysterious forces at work in the drama of deviance, respecting that version of common sense which focuses our attention on what we can see plainly as well as on those events and interests which require more subtle data-gathering and theoretical analysis.

At a second level, the interactionist approach shows sociologists that a major element in every aspect of the drama of deviance is the imposition of definitions—of situations, acts, and people—by those powerful enough or sufficiently legitimated to be able to do so. A full understanding requires the thorough study of those definitions and the processes by which they develop and attain legitimacy and taken-for-grantedness.

Both these levels of analysis give the interactionist approach, under present circumstances, a radical character. Interactionist analyses, by making moral entrepreneurs (as well as those they seek to control) objects of study, violate society's hierarchy of credibility. They question the monopoly on the truth and the "whole story" claimed by those in positions of power and authority. They suggest that we need to discover the truth about allegedly deviant phenomena for ourselves, instead of relying on the officially certified accounts which ought to be enough for any good citizen. They adopt a relativistic stance toward the accusations and definitions of deviance made by respectable people and constituted authority, treating them as the raw material of social science analysis rather than as statements of unquestioned moral truths.

Interactionist analyses of deviant phenomena become radical in a final sense by being treated as radical by conventional authorities. When authorities, political and otherwise, wield power in part by obfuscation and mystification, a science which makes things clearer inevitably attacks the bases of that power. The authorities whose institutions and jurisdictions become the object of interactionist analyses attack those analyses for their "biases," their failure to accept traditional wisdom and values, their destructive effect on public order.[6]

These consequences of interactionist analysis complicate our moral position as scientists by the very act of clarifying what is going on in such moral arenas as courts, hospitals, schools, and prisons. They make it impossible to ignore the moral implications of our work. Even if we want to do that, those authorities who feel themselves under attack destroy the illusion of a neutral science by insisting that we are responsible for those implications—as, of course, we are.

This discussion of recent developments in deviance theory makes a beginning on a consideration of the moral import of contemporary sociology. We can make further progress on that knotty problem by similar examinations in such other fields of sociology as the study of educational institutions, health services, the military, industry, and business—indeed, in *all* the other areas in which sociological study clarifies the activities of people and institutions, and thereby influences our moral evaluations of them.

6. For a fuller discussion of the notion of radical sociology, see Becker and Horowitz, 1972.

References

Akers, Ronald L. 1968. "Problems in the Sociology of Deviance: Social Definitions and Behavior." *Social Forces* 46 (June): 455–465.

Alvarez, Rodolfo. 1968. "Informal Reactions to Deviance in Simulated Work Organizations: A Laboratory Experiment." *American Sociological Review* 33 (December): 895–912.

Becker, Howard S. 1963. Outsiders: Studies in the Sociology of Deviance. New York: The Free Press of Glencoe.

Becker, Howard S. 1967. "Whose Side Are We On?" *Social Problems* 14 (Winter): 239–247.

Becker, Howard S. and Irving Louis Horowitz. 1972. "Radical Politics and Sociological Research: Observations on Methodology and Ideology." *American Journal of Sociology* 78 (July): 48–66.

Becker, Howard S. and Mack, Raymond W. 1971. "Unobtrusive Entry and Accidental Access to Field Data." Unpublished paper presented at a conference on Methodological Problems in Comparative Sociological Research, Institute for Comparative Sociology, Indiana University.

Biderman, Albert D. and Reiss, Albert J., Jr. 1967. "On Exploring the Dark Figure." *The Annals* 374 (November): 1–15.

Bittner, Egon and Garfinkel, Harold. 1967. " 'Good' Organizational Reasons for 'Bad' Clinic Records." In Harold Garfinkel, Studies in Ethnomethodology. Englewood Cliffs, New Jersey: Prentice-Hall.

Blumer, Herbert. 1966. "Sociological Implications of the Thought of George Herbert Mead." *American Journal of Sociology* 71 (March): 535–544.

Blumer, Herbert. 1967. "Threats from Agency-Determined Research: The Case of Camelot." In Irving Louis Horowitz, editor, The Rise and Fall of Project Camelot. Cambridge: M.I.T. Press. Pp. 153–174.

Blumer, Herbert. 1969. "The Methodological Position of Symbolic Interactionism." In his Symbolic Interactionism. Englewood Cliffs, New Jersey: Prentice-Hall. Pp. 1–60.

Bordua, David. 1967. "Recent Trends: Deviant Behavior and Social Control." *The Annals* 369 (January): 149–163.

Cicourel, Aaron. 1968. The Social Organization of Juvenile Justice. New York: John Wiley and Sons.

Cohen, Albert K. 1965. "The Sociology of the Deviant Act: Anomie Theory and Beyond." *American Sociological Review* 30 (February): 5–14.

Cohen, Albert K. 1966. Deviance and Control. Englewood Cliffs, New Jersey: Prentice-Hall.

Cohen, Albert K. 1968. "Deviant Behavior." In International Encyclopedia of the Social Sciences, Volume 4, pp. 148–155.

Cohen, Stanley, editor. 1971. Images of Deviance. Baltimore: Penguin Books.

Dalton, Melville. 1959. Men Who Manage. New York: John Wiley and Sons.

Douglas, Jack D. 1967. The Social Meanings of Suicide. Princeton: Princeton University Press.

Douglas, Jack D. 1970. "Deviance and Respectability: The Social Construction of Moral Meanings." In Jack D. Douglas, editor, Deviance and Respectability. New York: Basic Books, Inc.

Edel, Abraham. 1955. Ethical Judgment: The Uses of Science in Ethics. New York: The Free Press of Glencoe.

Erikson, Kai T. 1966. Wayward Puritans. New York: John Wiley and Sons.

Galtung, Johan. 1965. "Los Factores Socioculturales y el Desarrollo de la Sociologia en America Latina." *Revista Latinoamericana de Sociologia* 1 (March).

Garfinkel, Harold. 1967. Studies in Ethnomethodology. Englewood Cliffs, New Jersey: Prentice-Hall.

Gibbs, Jack. 1966. "Conceptions of Deviant Behavior: The Old and the New." *Pacific Sociological Review* 9 (Spring): 9–14.

Goode, Erich. 1970. The Marihuana Smokers. New York: Basic Books, Inc.

Gouldner, Alvin W. 1968. "The Sociologist as Partisan: Sociology and the Welfare State." *The American Sociologist* 3 (May): 103–116.

Gove, Walter. 1970a. "Societal Reaction as an Explanation of Mental Illness: An Evaluation." *American Sociological Review* 35 (October): 873–884.

Gove, Walter. 1970b. "Who Is Hospitalized: A Critical Review of Some Sociological Studies of Mental Illness." *Journal of Health and Social Behavior* 11 (December): 294–303.

Gusfield, Joseph. 1963. Symbolic Crusade. Urbana: University of Illinois Press.

Habenstein, Robert W., editor. 1970. Pathways to Data: Field Methods for Studying Ongoing Social Organizations. Chicago: Aldine Publishing Co.

Horowitz, Irving Louis and Liebowitz, Martin. 1968. "Social Deviance and Political Marginality: Toward a Redefinition of the Relation Between Sociology and Politics." *Social Problems* 15 (Winter): 280–296.

Humphreys, Laud. 1970. Tearoom Trade. Chicago: Aldine Publishing Co.

Kaplan, John. 1970. Marihuana: The New Prohibition. New York: World Publishing Co.

Katz, Jack. 1972. "Deviance, Charisma and Rule-Defined Behavior." *Social Problems* 20 (Winter): 186–202.

Kitsuse, John I. 1962. "Societal Reaction to Deviant Behavior: Problems of Theory and Method." *Social Problems* 9 (Winter): 247–256.

Kitsuse, John I. and Cicourel, Aaron V. 1963. "A Note on the Uses of Official Statistics." *Social Problems* 11 (Fall): 131–139.

Lemert, Edwin M. 1951. Social Pathology. New York: McGraw-Hill Book Co.

Lemert, Edwin M. 1972. Human Deviance, Social Problems, and Social Control. 2nd edition. Englewood Cliffs, New Jersey: Prentice-Hall, Inc.

Liazos, Alexander. 1972. "The Poverty of the Sociology of Deviance: Nuts, Sluts, and Preverts." *Social Problems* 20 (Winter): 103–120.

Lindesmith, Alfred R. 1968. Addiction and Opiates. Chicago: Aldine Publishing Co.

Lorber, Judith. 1967. "Deviance and Performance: The Case of Illness." *Social Problems* 14 (Winter): 302–310.

Mankoff, Milton. 1970. "Power in Advanced Capitalist Society." *Social Problems* 17 (Winter): 418–430.

Mankoff, Milton. 1968. "On Alienation, Structural Strain, and Deviancy." *Social Problems* 16 (Summer): 114–116.

Matza, David. 1969. Becoming Deviant. Englewood Cliffs, New Jersey: Prentice-Hall, Inc.

Mead, George Herbert. 1934. Mind, Self and Society. Chicago: University of Chicago Press.

Messinger, Sheldon L. 1969. Strategies of Control. Unpublished Ph.D. dissertation, University of California at Los Angeles.

Mills, C. Wright. 1956. The Power Elite. New York: Oxford University Press.

Ray, Marsh. 1961. "The Cycle of Abstinence and Relapse among Heroin Addicts." *Social Problems* 9 (Fall): 132–140.

Roy, Donald. 1954. "Efficiency and the 'Fix': Informal Intergroup Relations in a Piecework Machine Shop." *American Journal of Sociology* 60 (November): 255–266.

Scheff, Thomas J. 1966. Being Mentally Ill. Chicago: Aldine Publishing Co.

Schur, Edwin M. 1969. "Reactions to Deviance: A Critical Assessment." *American Journal of Sociology* 75 (November): 309–322.

Selby, Henry. Not Every Man Is Humble. Unpublished manuscript.

Short, James F., Jr. and Strodtbeck, Fred L. 1965. Group Process and Gang Delinquency. Chicago: University of Chicago Press.

Skolnick, Jerome. 1969. The Politics of Protest. New York: Ballantine Books.

Strauss, Anselm L. *et al.* 1964. Psychiatric Ideologists and Institutions. New York: The Free Press of Glencoe.

Szasz, Thomas S. 1965. Psychiatric Justice. New York: MacMillan.

Szasz, Thomas S. 1967. "The Psychiatrist as Double Agent." *Trans-Action* 4 (October): 16–24.

Tannenbaum, Frank. 1938. Crime and the Community. New York: Ginn and Co.

Index

213